Planning and Observation of Children under Three

The most rapid and significant phase of development occurs in the first three years of a child's life. The *Supporting Children from Birth to Three* series focuses on the care and support of the very youngest children. Each book takes a key aspect of working with this age group and gives clear and detailed explanations of relevant theories together with practical examples to show how such theories translate into good working practice.

Effective planning and observation are fundamental to young children's learning and development. Learning opportunities for children need to be relevant for their age group, realistic and challenging.

Drawing on recent research, this book explains why the planning cycle is so important and looks at the links between observation, planning and assessment. Taking a holistic approach to supporting children's learning, it shows how a range of observation strategies can provide insight into children's social, emotional, physical and cognitive development and practically demonstrates how practitioners can develop appropriate planning and observation techniques for babies and toddlers.

Features include:

* clear explanation of relevant theories
* case studies and examples of good practice
* focus points for readers
* questions for reflective practice.

Providing a wealth of practical ideas and activities, this handy text explores all aspects of planning and observation with the under-threes to help practitioners ensure effective outcomes for the youngest children in their care.

Helen Bradford is an Early Years Tutor on the Early Years and Primary PGCE course at the Faculty of Education, University of Cambridge, UK. Her previous publications for Routledge include: *Communication, Language and Literacy* (Fulton, 2008) *Bears* (Fulton, 2006) *Woodland Creatures* (Fulton, 2005) and *Ourselves* (Fulton, 2005).

Supporting Children from Birth to Three
Series Editor: Sandy Green

The most rapid and significant phase of development occurs in the first three years of a child's life. The *Supporting Children from Birth to Three* series focuses on the care and support of the youngest children. Each book takes a key aspect of working with this age group and gives clear and detailed explanations of relevant theories together with practical examples to show how such theories translate into good working practice.

Each title in this series includes the following features:

- clear explanation of relevant theories
- case studies and examples of good practice
- focus points for readers
- questions for reflective practice.

Collectively, the series provides practical ideas and activities to help practitioners to develop appropriate indoor and outdoor environments, to appreciate the importance of the planning cycle and to gain a better understanding of all aspects of babies and infants' well-being.

Titles in this series include:

Appropriate Environments for Children under Three
Helen Bradford

Planning and Observation of Children under Three
Helen Bradford

The Wellbeing of Children under Three
Helen Bradford

Planning and Observation of Children under Three

Helen Bradford

Routledge
Taylor & Francis Group

LONDON AND NEW YORK

First published 2012
by Routledge
2 Park Square, Milton Park, Abingdon, Oxon OX14 4RN

Simultaneously published in the USA and Canada
by Routledge
711 Third Avenue, New York, NY 10017

Routledge is an imprint of the Taylor & Francis Group, an informa business

British Library Cataloguing in Publication Data
A catalogue record for this book is available from the British Library

Library of Congress Cataloging in Publication Data
Bradford, Helen.
Planning and observation of children under three / Helen Bradford.
    p. cm. – (Supporting children from birth to three)
  Includes bibliographical references and index.
  1. Early childhood education–Planning. 2. Child development.
  I. Title.
  LB1139.23.B735 2012
  372.21–dc23   2011030074

ISBN: 978-0-415-61267-8 (hbk)
ISBN: 978-0-415-61268-5 (pbk)
ISBN: 978-0-203-13590-7 (ebk)

Typeset in Optima by
HWA Text and Data Management, London

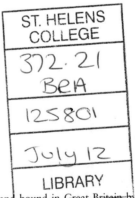

MIX
Paper from
responsible sources
FSC® C004839

Printed and bound in Great Britain by
CPI Antony Rowe, Chippenham, Wiltshire

Contents

Figures

Tables

Introduction

Planning and Observation for Children under Three is one of a series of three books providing supportive and accessible material for those who work with the very youngest age range, from birth to three years. The premise for all three books is twofold; all babies and young children under three are 1) social beings and 2) competent learners from birth. The other two titles in the series are:

- *Appropriate Environments for Children under Three*, and;
- *The Wellbeing of Children under Three*.

The books are designed for all early years professionals and adults working with babies and children under three in their early years settings who are seeking ideas on how to optimise best practice using the space and resources they have available to them. The books explore some of the theories and principles behind good practice in each of the title areas outlined. *Planning and Observation for Children under Three* includes examples from practice, and exercises for readers, as well as a chapter with suggestions for reviewing setting practice, including staff development. The series is written from the perspective of the early years practitioner as someone who is in a privileged position to work with children from birth to three; someone who is able to see and respond to each child they encounter as the idiosyncratic individual that they inevitably are. Thus how can the early years practitioner working with such a perspective best meet every child's needs? How can every child be best supported as they evolve and develop to make sense of the world around them?

The books take a reflective, child-led approach where good practice begins with an understanding of child development, appropriate responses, honest evaluation, and ongoing discourse amongst practitioners. *Planning and*

Observation for Children under Three relies on a staff team who can work together collaboratively to develop ways of providing high-quality learning environments so that all the children in their care feel secure and happy and are able to thrive. Feeling secure and happy and being able to thrive mean paradoxically that children must also feel able to take risks appropriate to their stages of development; to explore, inquire, enquire, and experiment as their knowledge and understanding of the environments they inhabit grows. As they develop a language, or meta-language, that enables them to communicate in and navigate those environments, and as they develop the physical and creative skills necessary to experience the exciting and intriguing spaces that unfold themselves before them, so children begin a journey of understanding that will support and equip them for life ahead. According to the Early Childhood Forum 'it [pre-school experience] is a crucial time in children's development … pre-school experience provides many of the building blocks for the rest of their lives.' A key message of this book therefore is that appropriate planning and observation play a pivotal role in supporting and extending children's development and learning.

All the chapters in this book build on each other whilst containing the same core messages. Chapter 1 outlines a discussion of 'curriculum' in relation to babies and children under three which includes a broader perspective than that of a framework which is merely subject-based. A quality curriculum must include a significant element of appropriate developmental care. Chapter 2 gives an overview of considerations behind the notion of planning for this age group; what are we planning for and indeed, why plan at all? Examples of, and suggestions for, planning are included as well as explanations of key terminology. Chapter 3 looks at successful planning in the context of a secure background knowledge of the developing child, making links between theory and appropriate practice within six key areas of learning; cognitive, brain, language, social and emotional, and physical development, as well as learning through play. Chapter 4 investigates observation as a tool for gathering key information about a child and what the purpose of this might be. Chapter 5 draws planning and observation together to look at what can be done to develop appropriate planning and observation techniques for children aged between 0–3 within the context of the early years environment, and considers what can be learnt from global perspectives. Chapter 6 suggests ways for a setting to review current practice in relation to planning and observation with exercises to support ongoing setting development. Chapter 7 draws threads of thinking together, summarising the main lines of thinking throughout the book.

Considerations for the curriculum: assuring quality for babies and children under three

Beginning with a discussion on the definition of curriculum in relation to babies and children under three, this chapter then moves on to look at an overview of the structural characteristics of early child care and education (Wertfein et al. 2009) and what their effects are on the quality of provision. Structural characteristics include factors such as group size, staff understanding of the learning and developmental needs of the age group they are caring for, and preparation (including planning) time. This chapter further considers how a setting can ensure that quality of provision is in fact an outcome of planned practice. Finally, the chapter asks what evidence there is to suggest that the resources a setting has, including practitioners (staff), as well as the environment (setting), and the means available to cater for children in their care (toys, care equipment, food), are going to best support the very specific needs of babies and children under three.

A quality curriculum

An outcome of the EPPE study (Sylva et al. 2010) suggests that effective early years settings will benefit most from staff who are familiar with the curriculum and who have expert knowledge on how small children learn. When we think of the word 'curriculum', there is a tendency to focus on a child's learning of different subjects; what they need to know and be taught within a certain curriculum area such as mathematics or literacy, for example. Eventually the child will achieve certain prescribed goals or outcomes and can then move on – to learn even more! In recent years many countries in Europe have revised existing early childhood curricula or introduced new frameworks which have acknowledged and focussed on the importance of what happens in relation to care experiences (both at home and in early years settings) during a child's formative years (see Sylva *et al.* 2010, for example).

As a result of such lines of thinking, significantly augmented and supported by current, up-to-date research evidence, the profile of the 0–3 age range has been significantly raised over recent years and is now firmly embedded as part of vital and inclusive early years best practice. An example of this has been the 0–3 curriculum in England which is currently covered under the umbrella of a statutory framework called the Early Years Foundation Stage (DfES 2007), for use with children from birth to five years. The Early Years Foundation Stage is an amalgamation of two previous documents; the non-statutory Birth to Three Matters Framework launched in 2002 and the statutory Curriculum Guidance for the Foundation Stage (DfEE 2005) for children aged between three and five years old. The fact that the Birth to Three Matters Framework was non-statutory speaks volumes for the earlier assumptions made in relation to this age group.

Because so much more is now known and understood in terms of related research about the social, emotional and physical developmental areas of babies and children under three, an appropriate curriculum must therefore encompass far more than mere areas of subject learning (although these are important), in that this age group needs to be cared for and nurtured at very much a grass roots level. A range of specific needs must be met; therefore what kind of curriculum should be in place in an early years setting to facilitate and ensure appropriate developmental and learning experiences? Nyland (2000) argues that it is everyday experiences which are the curriculum of the early years; the definition of 'curriculum' must therefore further extend to a much wider range of elements in the setting in which babies and children under three come to for care and how practitioners respond to them as individuals. Beneficial outcomes for children in child care are associated with settings that provide nurturance and support for early learning and development (Snow and Van Hemel 2008). Higher quality child care is related to advanced cognitive, language and pre-academic child outcomes (Burchinal *et al.* 1996; NICHD 2006). How can such beneficial and advanced outcomes be ensured? To put it another way in the context of the title of this book, how can high-quality care experiences be planned for babies and children under three with such outcomes in mind? Looking at the curriculum in this way might make it appear unfathomable – where on earth does the practitioner start? However, I would like to argue that such a curriculum presents a sensible and achievable picture of cohesion and strength and makes perfect sense when looked at in such a holistic way.

It is interesting to note that after beginning to write this book and draft this first chapter, the current Early Years Foundation Stage was undergoing a thorough evaluation and review following a change of government in 2010 in the United Kingdom. The review begins by stating that;

> The earliest years in a child's life are absolutely critical. There is overwhelming international evidence that foundations are laid in the first years of life which, if weak, can have a permanent and detrimental impact on children's longer term development. A child's future choices, attainment, wellbeing, happiness and resilience are profoundly affected by the quality of the guidance, love and care they receive during these first years.
>
> (Tickell 2011, p.2)

To this end, Tickell (2011) proposes that the Early Years Foundation Stage be restructured to focus on three overriding developmental areas; communication and language, personal, social and emotional development, and physical development. The crux of the argument behind Tickell's proposal is that it is these three areas which, quite rightly, encompass the 'essential foundations for healthy development, for positive attitudes to relationships and learning, and for progress in key skills such as reading and writing' (Tickell 2011, p.20). The review further proposes a required written summary of every child's development between the ages of 24–36 months in each of these three overarching areas. Summaries of children's progress will be written by early years practitioners, including childminders. It is this open, shared report that will then be used to identify those children whose progress may be lacking in any or all of the key developmental areas and additional support allocated. The focus here is clear; the child's developmental needs first and foremost and an emphasis on getting the foundations right to enable future learning to take place for every individual child.

It is logical to develop lines of thinking further in relation to an appropriate curriculum and appropriate care before every early years setting, in England at least, wonders at the extent of how current practice might have to change. Surely it is more a case of looking at existing current (and good) established practice and evaluating this in the light of proposed change. Not everything will need to change; indeed this book is about reviewing, evaluating and implementing suggested changes in probably already established practice in relation to planning and observation, processes which are an inherent feature of good, reflective early years practice.

Quality provision within the early years setting

Wüstenberg and Schneider (2008, cited in Wertfein *et al.* 2009, p.20) argue that there are seven important quality indicators for the daily care of babies and children under three. These are as follows:

1   *The individual adjustment process.* The individual adjustment process is about how every child is supported to settle in in the setting. It is important to remember that whilst a setting might have a broad overarching policy to introduce families and their children to the care environment, Wüsternberg and Schneider emphasise the *individual* in their concept of the adjustment process. This is therefore a process which should be reviewed on an ongoing basis in relation to every individual child as there will be periods, for example after illness or holidays, that have the potential to unsettle an otherwise settled child.

2   *A familiar person (or key worker) who the child accepts and responds to.* The key worker provides continuity of care for an individual child and acts as a key link between home and the setting, ensuring close communication with parents is maintained. This relationship means that vital information can be taken into account when planning for those individual children, such as particular interests, favourite nursery rhymes or picture books, and care routines. This is the kind of information which will help provide continuity of care between the home and the setting and further extend and support the concept of the individual adjustment process described above.

3   *Warm and stable relationships between practitioner and child.* All children like to be liked (Parker-Rees 2007) and it goes without saying that all children respond to love, kindness and understanding. For those children who might have a more impoverished home life in this respect, the setting, through providing high-quality care, plays a key role (Sylva *et al.* 2010).

4   *Orientation towards a child's needs, interests and well-being.* (See in particular point 2 above). Oberhuemer (2005) argues that there is now a general consensus that early childhood curricula should meet the child's needs and interests; in turn supporting healthy well-being.

5   *Nurturing relationships, healthy nutrition and a clear, daily routine.* Nurturing relationships, healthy nutrition and a clear, daily routine encompass a strong emphasis on a personal, social and emotional element of early years curricula.

6   *Materials and activities which stimulate the child's exploratory drive.* It is important to resource the setting appropriately, or at least to review provision to ensure that current resources are being used to the optimum effect to satisfy the curiosity and inquisitive nature of babies and children under three.

7   *A local network of resources and specialists for both children and their parents.* Parents of babies and children under three often need support. Not only does a key worker play a significant role in supporting parents, but settings must consider their range of provision extending to the particular needs of the community they serve. These might include for example classes they offer, or specialist talks they arrange, important notices displayed clearly where parents will see them, and contact numbers for local organisations and services.

Whilst each indicator has only been briefly expanded above, it is with these in mind that a discussion of an appropriate or quality curriculum can be pursued. The final quality indicator above is worthy of some consideration at this point and has important implications for a setting's curriculum. Taking England as an example, legislation regulating Sure Start Children's Centres is designed to help improve outcomes for young children through targeted early years provision in their area. The rationale behind this approach supports an overarching aim to narrow the gap between those children who do well and those who do not (Alexander 2010). If we think about this in relation to the wider curriculum, the concept of 'provision in their area' is important, because it recognises the fact that in this country at least people live in often culturally diverse communities. A quality curriculum must therefore be interpreted in a flexible way to ensure that early years provision is tailored accordingly to meet the specific needs of each community; an approach important for the identity of each and every early years setting which should further be perceived as a community in itself. It is also worth noting at this point that Wüstenberg and Schneider's quality indicator does not restrict itself to rich and poor, in that it applies to *all* early years settings and the community they serve, regardless of socio-economic well-being.

Reflecting on current practice

1   What do you as a setting offer that is unique in the community?
2   What are the needs of the community you serve?
3   What do you currently offer to support those needs?
4   What do you currently provide beyond day-to-day care for babies and children under three to support the needs of the parents coming to your setting?
5   Is there anything that you could plan to implement to enhance current provision?
6   How will you as a setting evaluate or assess the outcomes of such new initiatives?

A foundation from which to plan: the individual learning needs of babies and children under three

Walsh and Gardner (2005) argue that the quality of an early years setting is principally determined by the way in which the learning and developmental needs of the main stakeholders, that is to say the children, are met. The focus, in this book at least, must then move to the individual child and to individual needs. What does this mean in practice in relation to planning concerns? In the first book of this series, 'Appropriate Environments for Babies and Children under Three', the following key areas for consideration with this unique age group were put forward. They are reproduced here, this time with suggested links to opportunities for planning.

1   *Supporting children to learn at their own pace*, or planning for careful progression. In order to be able to plan successfully for learning to take place at a child's own pace, a practitioner must be secure in their judgement of current ability levels; these are the foundations on which to build to ensure future progression. There is no value or mileage in giving children a twenty-piece jigsaw if they can only manage a six-piece tray puzzle, for example. We thus see that observation and assessment must be an integral part of the planning process.

2   *Following children's interests and enabling opportunities for (including planning for) those interests to be pursued within the learning environment.* Planning appropriately for any child is dependent on an in-depth knowledge of them as an individual. This means taking a holistic approach and looking at their specific emotional and developmental needs, developing appropriate planning to ensure successful outcomes that equate to progress. A beginning point might be to think about how to engage them in learning; what appeals to the child; trains? dinosaurs? The fascinating conkers they found on the way to the setting that morning? Table 2.1 (p.19) looks at a week's planning that includes developing activities following children's interests.

3   *Supporting children to develop a view of themselves as happy, enthusiastic learners.* Again, opportunities for planning are relevant here in relation to a child's social and emotional development. Small steps are key, planned for within the context of a secure knowledge of child development on the part of the practitioner, for example singing nursery rhymes or pointing to and naming facial features when changing a nappy. Showing interest in this way will ensure that the child feels valued, liked, and cared for.

4   *Encouraging children to see the world as an interesting place.* An understanding of how babies and children under three make sense of their world is important. Children are born with an innate sense of curiosity, thus what can the early years practitioner plan to stimulate and maximise such curiosity based on what is known about a particular child's developmental needs and their particular interests? Whether in the pushchair or by foot, taking children on a walk to explore the outdoor environment at the setting and pointing out and talking about all the interesting flowers and plants is a good idea. Look at colours and features such as shapes. If a child is in a pushchair, position them so that they can experience as much as possible through the senses of touch and sight. Model opportunities available such as digging in mud. Taking young children by the hand is another way of helping them to develop the confidence to eventually explore independently; encourage them to feel the texture of the grass or listen to the sound both your sets of footsteps make on different surfaces such as gravel or concrete. Once children are familiar with the environment they will begin to explore it for themselves. Follow their explorations and provide points of interest that will engage them such as hiding dinosaurs in the bushes. Help them develop a story as to how they got there!

5   *Offering the security of warm relationships, perhaps through a key worker system which links individual practitioners with individual children and their parents or carers.* Knowing a child extremely well will have a subsequent

influence on the appropriateness of planned opportunities and activities throughout the time the child spends at the setting. This will of course extend to planning for personal care, incorporating routines for nappy changing, sleep, and regular mealtimes for example, discussed in further detail in Chapter 5 (NB. If a key worker system is in place at your setting it is worth considering an appropriate contingency plan for a child when their key worker is not there).

6   *Expressing affection through words, body language, and cuddles.* Parker-Rees (2007) looked at reciprocated exchanges between 'attentive adults and very young children', arguing that the adult provides a 'social mirror' (p.7) for the child's earliest attempts at communication, exploration and developing understanding of their world:

> because infants enjoy the companionship and familiarity associated with seeing their own behaviour returned to them with interest, they reward attentive adults with smiles, laughter and infectious joy, shaping the adults' behaviour even as their own behaviour is shaped by the adults' editing.
>
> (Parker-Rees 2007, pp.8-9)

It takes a certain kind of person to work with babies and children under three; you must absolutely love what you do! Understanding that you are engaging in a two-way reciprocal relationship, even with the youngest of babies, is crucial.

7   *Allocating time to personal care, appreciating a child's gradual development of self-help skills.* Regular routines for personal care for young children are not something to hurry through so that they can be moved on to activities viewed as 'educational', a line of thinking discussed earlier in this chapter. Physical care is an important element of the time shared by the practitioner with babies and children under three. Planning for gradual independence is key; and again will be successfully based on the practitioner's knowledge of child development in terms of expectation with regard to potential outcomes (can I expect two-year-old Ella for example to put her wellington boots on by herself to go outside, or will she need me to help her?), as well as knowledge of an individual child's current achievements.

8   *Developing listening skills to understand what children are feeling and what it is they need from their early years experience.* Developing child-led planning skills is essential to good early years practice, based on secure knowledge and understanding of the developmental and learning needs

Figure 1.1 Playing and learning together

of the age group. When a child cries persistently for example, what is your response? Do you ignore them, or ask them to shut up out of frustration? Or do you check that their nappy is clean, that they have a drink, give them a cuddle to reassure them, talking gently to them to try to help them settle, take their temperature? Do you talk to the parents to see whether there may be any underlying reason for the crying such as teething? Learn what children are saying through the noises and sounds that they make.

9   *Supporting children to play and, as they become older, supporting them to play considerately with others and to take care of their play/learning environments.* Planning to facilitate learning through play is another key element of best practice. Learning through play will be discussed further in Chapter 3. Part of developing independence involves children, and this includes very young children, learning what the 'rules' are in relation to taking care of their play and learning environment. Practitioners involved in the very early, formative years of children's lives, working from a clear starting point of established commitment and expertise will be able to constantly find opportunities to link experiences in with planning for personal, social, emotional, and physical development. Reading a book with two or three children is an example of such an opportunity where the children have to 'share' the practitioner; this may be hard for some, especially an only child doted on at home and used to getting their own way! Learning to play

happily alongside peers is an important element of a child's personal, social and emotional development. Asking a child to return a book to the book box will help develop their skill in moving from sitting to standing, walking and accuracy in placing the book back in the box. At first they will need the practitioner to support them by holding their hand to enable them to balance – but eventually, as their stability and physical skills develop, will be able to put the book back by themselves. Establishing this kind of routine early on in a child's life will help develop strong foundations in relation to behavioural expectations.

Chapter conclusion

This chapter has outlined several key points to be considered in relation to a rationale for appropriate planning for babies and children under three. It began by considering the definition of what is meant by the term 'curriculum' and the implications of what this might mean for this age group. The chapter is based on an understanding of their very specific needs, which by default suggests that an appropriate curriculum must extend beyond so-called traditional subject areas. The chapter looks at how to assure quality of provision for babies and children under three using Wüstenberg and Schneider's (2008, cited in Wertfein et al. 2009, p.20) quality indicators as the basis for providing a helpful foundation for beginning to think about planning. Finally key areas for consideration in relation to appropriate care have been put forward and linked directly to opportunities for planning. Each consideration and deliberation is based upon the holistic premise of the child as a unique individual.

Why plan?
An overview

This chapter uncovers key principles behind planning and discusses an overview of what constitutes good, supportive, appropriate planning for babies and children under three.

To plan or not to plan: principles behind planning

Planning begins with following a curriculum, statutory or otherwise. In this respect it is about organisation of input according to some pre-defined or pre-described criteria. Plans also act as a guide to managing the learning/care environment (the indoor and outdoor space for example, including their organisation and layout); they allow the practitioner to consider strategies and methods they will use to enhance learning.

If we go back to two-year-old Ella as our example again, trying to put on her Wellington boots to go outside; what would the expectations be? You as the practitioner, want her to put on her boots as part of an overall objective of dressing appropriately for the outdoor weather say. What does this actually mean? Do you expect her to find the boots and bring them to you so that you can help her to put them on? Do you want her to have a go at putting them on herself with the risk that she may put them on the wrong feet and feel uncomfortable? Can you expect her to know right from left at this young age? Do you therefore intend to place the boots in front of her in the right way so that when she sits to put them on she has a much better chance of getting them on the right feet straightaway? Will you be modelling putting wellington boots

Figure 2.1 Whatever the weather: investigating outdoors

on alongside her so that you both put one boot on together at a time? After all of that you will then still need to get her to put on her coat, hat and gloves! If she wears a one-piece ski suit-type coat to go outside in, then it is no good putting the boots on first! Planning is about organisation and an opportunity for thinking things through. Timing and pace are real factors in the process – how much time should you realistically allow for Ella to get ready to go outside as part of the overall learning experience? And does it really matter how much time it takes when getting ready to go outside in the cold involves so many potential learning opportunities for her? Here are some of them:

- developing self-esteem;
- developing a 'can do' perspective;
- developing independence;
- developing hand-eye coordination;
- developing self-help skills;
- developing higher order thinking skills;
- developing motivational skills;
- developing concentration;

- developing well-being;
- developing knowledge and understanding of the seasons and/or weather;
- experiencing the sensory impact of cold weather on the body.

Activity

Thinking through the example of Ella getting ready to go outside, write a qualifying sentence for each of the bullet points above showing how she is developing each skill throughout this particular scenario.

Can you think of anything else she is learning from this experience?

Clearly planning benefits all children, however whilst allowing for organisational elements to be thought through, plans should ultimately always be seen as a set of guidelines. They are flexible, working documents, not blueprints that must be followed to the letter. It is the confident, well-informed early years practitioner who knows when a plan is not working and adapts input or support accordingly. It is perhaps helpful to picture plans as designs; designs change and in the same way plans may also need to be changed and adapted when children do not respond in the way the practitioner might expect. Picture yourself as a designer, implementer and facilitator, setting out various elements or components for the children in your care that need to ultimately fit together, but which may not fit together as originally thought. The elements or components may therefore need to change according to the child, their response, and the developmental progress they are making.

What is the practitioner planning for? Key elements of planning for babies and children under three

Essentially the early years practitioner is planning for learning and development to take place. For babies and children under three, planning needs to take into account specific, individual care needs. It is still helpful to begin by looking at planning under the umbrella of long-, medium-, and short-term planning; the usual, embedded pattern throughout education. Long-term planning for this age group is not actually necessary in that it is impossible to predict what a young child may be interested in or what rate of progress they may make even over a six-month period. Whilst this may feel liberating, planning will still need to take place! What is the starting point for the early years practitioner therefore? Planning must essentially be undertaken from the starting-point of a secure knowledge of child development (explored in greater detail in the next chapter).

Medium-term plans (monthly or half termly if your setting follows a typical academic school year in England) involve the setting's 'continuous provision'. These are the resources available for children to access independently, where there is no pre-identified outcome or learning intention. This is not to say that children do not learn when they access this type of resource; far from it. The skilled early years practitioner will be able to map outcomes and achievements through observation of children's play, for example, following the choices they make. A setting's continuous provision should reflect children's interests and support areas of development significant to individual children within the age range over this short period of time. Table 2.1 (p.19) shows an example of continuous provision.

Short-term planning involves weekly documents (guidelines remember, not blueprints!) which should reflect a mix of adult-led and child-initiated activity. Considerations for short-term planning include:

- *Children's intended learning and development* – key questions to ask include:
  - What do they already know?
  - What do I want the children to learn?
  - What could they learn?

- *Response to observation and children's interests* – key questions to ask include:
  - What are the children learning through the choices they make?
  - How are the children building on that they have already learnt?
  - How can children be supported to learn through utilising what interests them?
  - What could be planned next to further support learning through building on this particular interest?

- *Resources* – key questions to ask include:
  - What can the setting provide that will appropriately support learning?
  - Is there anything in the budget to support the provision of additional resources?

- Can we appeal to parents and carers for resources? (An example of this might be asking for unwanted costume jewellery, or asking for milk bottle tops for the older children in the setting).

- *Differentiation (including support and challenge)* – key questions to ask include:
  - What resources (including adult support) can the setting provide to support individual success?
  - How will that success be achieved?
  - How well do I know the individual child so that differentiation will be accurate?
  - How can I get to know the individual child well so that differentiation will be accurate?

- *Focused activities (adult-led)* – key questions to ask include:
  - What do I want the children to learn from/through this activity?
  - Is the activity purposeful? How do I know?
  - Is the activity meaningful? How do I know?
  - Is the activity age-appropriate? How do I know?

- *Adult roles* – key questions to ask include:
  - Is everyone involved today clear on their role (s)?
  - Has time been planned in to talk to everyone involved so that they know what the expectations are?
  - Is everyone familiar with processes for recording observations/recording outcomes?
  - How will feedback be ensured?

- *Key vocabulary* – key questions to ask include:
  - Has key vocabulary been carefully thought through?
  - Has *all* key vocabulary been included? Look again on your plan!

- *The indoor, and outdoor environment, and continuous provision* – key questions to ask include:
  - Where does the activity/intended learning take place?
  - Why is this area of the setting the best place for it?
  - Have all three areas been carefully and appropriately planned for?
  - Do I need to undertake any risk assessments?

- *Time and opportunity for observation, evaluation and assessment* – key questions to ask include:
    - Has time and opportunity for observation, evaluation and assessment been planned in to the day?
    - Is equal weight given to observing learning in the outdoor as well as the indoor area? Do notebooks/Post-its/clipboards go out into the garden/outdoor area with key workers to record immediate observations?
    - Following observations having been made, will there be time for collaborative discussion on certain children?

- *Next step:* – key questions to ask include:
    - How do I know what the next steps should be?
    - What do my observations tell me?
    - What do my evaluations tell me?
    - What do my assessments tell me?
    - What does the curriculum say should be the next steps in this area of learning?

Activity

Have a look at the examples of planning on the next few pages.
Is there anything else that you feel should be included in these plans?

Table 2.1 An example of short-term planning

A retrospective plan for a week of continuous provision (2–3 room) (adapted from DfES, 2007)

The planning sheet was organised so that the continuous provision for the week took into account a range of activities planned in response to the children's interests (**CI**) and those designed to ensure a balance of rich play experiences (**P**). The sheet shows the final activities that took place.

	Monday	Tuesday	Wednesday	Thursday	Friday
Sand	**CI:** Pine cones and greenery from the setting garden (in response to a child bringing in a large pine cone found at the weekend and several children showing an interest). NB It is useful to have a collection of pine cones as part of a range of setting 'natural resources'.	**CI:** Pine cones and conkers (in response to ongoing theme of child bringing some in to show). NB It is useful to have a box of conkers as a part of a range of setting 'natural resources'.	**P:** Buckets, spades and flags	**P:** Offer dry and wet sand in two separate trays with trucks in both (linked to interest in 'Duck in the Truck' this week)	**CI:** Mark making in wet sand: in addition to fingers: forks, twigs, lollipop sticks (in response to interest shown in mark making properties of wet sand using fingers yesterday)
Water	**CI:** Babies, shampoo bottles, soap, soap dishes, warm water and bubbles (in response to two children talking about their new sibling at home)	**P:** Plastic spiders, watering cans and guttering	**CI:** Plastic roadway, trucks and tubes (in response to enthusiasm when reading 'Duck in the Truck' on Monday)	**CI:** Tea set (in response to request from child the previous day)	**P:** Funnels, jugs and buckets

continued ...

Table 2.1 continued

	Monday	Tuesday	Wednesday	Thursday	Friday
Book Corner	P: 'Duck in the Truck' by Jez Alborough	P: 'Incy Wincy Spider' by Keith Chapman and Jack Tickle	CI: 'Duck in the Truck' by Jez Alborough (in response to demand!)	CI: Photo albums of children in the setting (with handwritten captions) in response to child request	P: 'Duck in the Truck' book and character puppets from Story Sack
Creative/ mark making/ messy	P: Paint and rollers	CI: Scarves and music (kept in wicker basket at floor level). In response to children hearing a nursery rhyme CD being played in the setting and asking to dance, extending to making their own music to dance to.	P: Green gloop	CI: Scissors, glue and magazines (in response to child having been doing this at home the previous evening)	P: This is the way we put on our clothes action song (sung to 'Here we go round the Mulberry Bush' tune)
Talk Area	P: Animal hand puppets	CI: Magnifying glasses and pine cones (in response to child being fascinated with the pine cones in the sand)	P: Range of textures to explore and talk about such as bubble wrap, cotton wool and material	P: Cameras and photographs	P: Shape sorter
Puzzles, games	P: Wooden stacking rings	P: Magnetic fishing game	CI: Outdoor skittles, chosen from a range of accessible games outside.	CI: Giant Connect Four and steps (in response to child having read 'Jack and the Beanstalk' with his key worker)	P: Range of wooden tray jigsaws

	Monday	Tuesday	Wednesday	Thursday	Friday
b	**P:** Stacking cardboard boxes	**P:** Stacking cardboard boxes and wooden blocks	**P/CI:** Stacking cardboard boxes, wooden blocks and cars (in response to child spontaneously adding cars for the garage he has made. Other children join in)	**P:** Duplo house and people	**CI:** Duplo house and people (in response to previous day's engagement with this resource)
Role Play	**CI:** Baking using play cooker and oven, saucepans, trays and utensils (in response to having baked with parents at the weekend)	**CI:** Baking, following on from previous day's response and one key worker reading 'The Gingerbread Man' with her children	**P:** Dressing up clothes	**CI:** Dressing teddies and dolls for a party (in response to child having received an invitation to a party)	**P/CI:** Dressing up clothes (following interest and delight shown from previous day)
Outside	**P:** Dinosaur feet – trail leading to large dinosaurs 'hiding' under a hedge	**P:** Digging with garden trug of tools and flowerpots (linked to investigating the properties of mud following 'Duck in the Truck' content and seeing how the children respond)	**CI:** Chalk directions (in response to a child wishing to create a treasure trail to a basket of shells)	**P:** Musical instruments and circle songs	**P:** Plastic wheeled vehicles and waterway
Snack	**P:** Pour own drink	**CI:** Helping to prepare snacks (asking key worker if they could help)	**P:** Inviting targeted children to help prepare snacks	**CI:** Counting out drinks as they are handed out	**P:** Choosing from a choice of snacks
Nappy Area	**P:** Range of mobiles over changing mats	**CI:** Naming parts of the body	**CI:** Talking about the day whilst being changed	**P:** Singing favourite rhymes	**P:** Listening to nursery rhyme CD and singing along together

Key terms for consideration when planning for babies and children under three

Areas of development and learning 1: the indoor environment

The indoor environment must be planned for with the unique and specific needs of babies and children under three in mind. The space available should promote comfort, stability and safety, as well as being somewhere where there is scope for even very young children to explore and take risks. Indoor environments will vary depending upon how your setting is organised; planning for a baby room will be very different to a 2–3 room, for example. The majority of planned experiences in the baby room will centre on everyday routines and children's individual care needs, whilst those practitioners based in the 2–3 room will be more able to incorporate a range of planned experiences based loosely on a theme.

Areas of development and learning 2: the outdoor environment

The outdoor environment is a natural space for learning and development where children can explore, experiment (including taking risks), have adventures, run, climb, shelter; the possibilities are endless! Settings will usually have designated areas outside for activities such as a quiet area (perhaps sheltered where babies can sleep), areas for playing in the sand and water, a digging area. There may be a climbing frame with a slide, along with wheeled equipment. A shed may be used as a role-play area; the Three Bears' Cottage for example, or a builder's office. There may be room for books and there should definitely be room for mark-making/writing opportunities to take place, for example buckets of water and paintbrushes, blackboards and chalks, paint, notebooks and pencils. Continuous provision should extend to the outdoor area, allowing a variety of potential experiences.

Continuous provision

These are the setting resources available to support areas of development for babies and children under three; resources to support children's interests, and for children to access independently as and when they become developmentally able. Whilst there does not have to be any pre-identified outcome or learning objective in relation to continuous provision, a broad range of potential outcomes will be evident to the experienced early years practitioner. Access to a collection of musical instruments for example will encourage a child's creative response and also their development of musical awareness and skills. For children to be able to access a setting's resources in this way allows for instances of child-initiated activities. Children may still be observed and assessed such that valid contributions may be made to their learning profile or a learning journey recorded. Potential observation and assessment opportunities arise out of:

1 allowing an element of free choice in this way, or
2 following a child's particular interest (see Simon's case study on p.48).

Child-initiated activities

Child-initiated or child-led activities 'require a more flexible perspective on planning' (Knight 2011, p.1). Child-initiated activities can develop in one of three ways:

1 through direct response to a request from a child for certain resources; requests can either be immediate or evolve during the session (a three-year-old in one of my nursery classes came in every day knowing *exactly* what resources he needed to fulfil his carefully thought through plans);
2 through a child choosing a resource that is appropriate for their agenda from a range of accessible resources available that day;
3 through practitioner response to a child's observed interactions and activities chosen.

The early years practitioner cannot plan a learning intention for a child-initiated activity, but through observation and adult support of children's play, it is possible to assess the learning that takes place. It is a good idea for early years practitioners to make notes to remind themselves to follow up children's self-initiated play. Appropriate resources can be added to the setting's continuous provision to this end so that children have the opportunity to revisit ideas and extend their learning in this way.

Adult-initiated activities

Adult-initiated activities are activities which are planned by the early years practitioner following a range of considerations based on knowledge of the curriculum, appropriate consideration of a child's developmental needs (including their language ability), and resources available in the setting. Planned learning intentions should be flexible so that the practitioner can pick up on the child's own learning agenda in response to the activity.

Learning journey

One way of recording a child's response to a specific experience is through a learning journey. A learning journey (see Figure 2.2) is both a formative and summative assessment document that records the progress of every child and feeds significantly into planning considerations. The key worker has the responsibility of planning for their key children on an individual level throughout each week. Effective planning is enabled through their knowledge of the child such as their responses, their interests, their likes, their dislikes, their achievements and their level of development. The learning journey provides specific information for future planning and support through building up a picture of a child's care, development, and learning.

Activity

What does Holly, Shania's key worker, know about child development in order to make the response to Shania's experience in Figure 2.2?

Is there anything else that could be added to the learning journey Next Steps?

Add in the links to your early years curriculum.

Figure 2.2 An example of a possible learning journey format (adapted from DfES, 2007).

Name	Shania
Age	One year
Key Worker	Holly

Observation/Notes:

Shania's mother came in to the setting this morning and told me that Shania had taken her first steps in the garden at the weekend. I took her outside and she took five steps towards me when I knelt facing her and holding out my hands. She noticed a flower nearby blowing in the wind. She pointed to it and walked towards it, taking three steps. She sat down to inspect it, using her nappy as a buffer as she dropped herself to the ground. I modelled smelling the flower, which she copied. We played 'my turn, your turn', one of her favourite games. After looking at and talking about the flower Shania reached out her arms to me to pick her up. I held her hands and encouraged her to stand up. She did and walked a few steps with me supporting her. I found a wheeled trolley for her and she stood up against it, holding the handle with both hands, thinking before she tried to push it and take a step at the same time. I helped her by holding the trolley for her and she moved forwards, somewhat unsteadily, but smiling and laughing in delight at what she was achieving.

Next Steps:

Materials and Resources	Activities and Experiences	Adult's Role
Trolley Wheeled toys Pram/dolly/teddy	Offer a selection of wheeled toys for Shania to push and use as part of her play as she develops her balance and confidence to combine walking and the skill of pushing	• Observe and record a dated diary of Shania's experiences. • Take photographs to add to learning journey. • Note whether she incorporates any further resources as part of the play experience and plan to include these in future planning. • Support physically as and when Shania requires. • Communicate with parents to see whether Shania's new walking skills can be supported in any other way at home.

Schema

Schema are 'repeatable patterns of behaviour, speech, representation and thought' (Nutbrown 2011, p.15) that children display in relation to their approach to a task or an activity or an experience that they encounter; they take what they know, their understanding and skills established and apply these to the situation at hand, using their schema as a way of problem- solving or coping in that situation. Nutbrown (2011) argues that early schemas seem to provide the basis for later learning. Such experiences can lead to the development of new lines of thinking for example, or the refinement of a skill that is partly established, or the beginnings of the development of a new skill. It is important to remember that a child's schema will be seen across a *range* of situations and actions. Table 2.2 shows examples of behavioural schema.

Table 2.2 Examples of behavioural schema

Schema	Possible behaviours
Transporting	A child may carry all the bricks from one place to another in a bag, the sand from the tray to the role play corner in a bucket, push a doll around in a toy pram.
Enveloping	A child may cover themselves with a flannel when washing, wrap a doll in a blanket, sit in the sand pit and cover their legs with sand, cover their whole painting with one colour.
Enclosure/containing	A child may put their thumb in and out of their mouth, fill up a empty containers of all kinds, climb into large boxes, sit in a play tunnel, build 'cages' with blocks.
Trajectory; diagonal/ vertical/horizontal	A child may gaze at your face, drop things from their cot, make arcs in their spilt food with their hand, play with the running water in the bathroom, climb up and jump on furniture, line up the cars, bounce and kick balls, throw.
Rotation	A child may be fascinated by the spinning washing machine, love anything on wheels, roll down a hill, enjoy spinning round or being swung round.
Connection	A child may distribute and collect objects to and from a practitioner, spend time joining the train trucks together, enjoy taping junk boxes together.
Positioning	A child may put things on their head, prefer their custard next to their sponge not over it, lie on the floor or under the table, walk around the edge of the sandpit.
Transforming	A child may add juice to their mashed potato, sand to the water tray, enjoy adding colour to cornflour, or making dough.

Your children and schema

Consider the above notion of children's schemas as an indication of a child's approach to and understanding in relation to learning. Are schemas already a consideration in your early years setting? If not, ask every practitioner to observe a chosen child over a period of time to see if schemas are evident. Remember that a child's schema must be seen across a *range* of situations and actions. Then consider the following questions:

* Are schemas as a way of looking at a child helpful for your setting?
* Why? Justify your response.
* Why not? Justify your response.

For more information on schemas look at:

C. Nutbrown, *Threads of thinking schemas and young children's learning* (4th edn), 2011, London: Sage.

S. Featherstone, *Again! Again! Understanding schemas in young children*, 2008, London: A&C Black.

Chapter conclusion

Additional lines of thinking must be taken into account when planning for babies and children under three because of their specific care needs. Some of those lines of thinking have been explored in this chapter to set the context for good, supportive and appropriate planning for the age group. What to include within long-, medium-, and short-term planning have been included for scrutiny by the reader. The language or terminology of planning for babies and children under three involves some key terms which have been explained and which will at times be referred to throughout the remaining chapters.

How do babies and children under three learn?

This chapter begins with a discussion of what learning means in relation to babies and children under three and what is included in early years curricula to support learning centred on a range of potential approaches. It is followed by an overview of six areas of developmental learning, each of which is outlined briefly and followed by examples of children's learning set in context and also in relation to an appropriately balanced curriculum. Implications for the early years practitioner in relation to planning are then outlined. Throughout the chapter the early years practitioner is encouraged to think carefully about their role and the basis from which they undertake planning.

Learning: a discussion and a context

Learning takes place when new knowledge and understanding about something is obtained or a new skill or behaviour is acquired as a result of experience. What babies and children under three 'need' to learn, as discussed in Chapter 1, is traditionally rooted in established early years curricula, a worldwide phenomenon. The Council for Curriculum, Examinations and Assessment (CCEA) in Northern Ireland argues that 'children learn best when all areas of an integrated, carefully planned, curriculum are implemented informally using methodologies that are interactive, practical and enjoyable' (2003, p.7). Despite the mention of a 'carefully planned curriculum', which might on first reading be construed as potentially restrictive, but should probably be rather interpreted as a facilitative framework within which development and learning take place, it has already been mentioned that in recent years, many countries in Europe have made strong efforts to revise existing early childhood curricula to particularly take into account the importance of formative experiences from birth. A key message from the above quote is rather one of flexibility and interpretation; note the immediate use of the term 'methodologies' rather than 'methodology'. Additionally, 'interactive, practical and enjoyable' suggest the potential for a range of creative and exciting planned responses in relation to what is known about each child and the progress they are making.

Development amongst babies and children under three is rapid but uneven. Every child is an individual with different learning needs and whilst it is possible to look at a broad spectrum of potential development, each will develop and learn in different ways and at different rates within that spectrum. In response, the early years practitioner needs to be flexible when planning according to individual children's stages of development. The need to take a flexible approach can further be exemplified through looking at the variety of ways in which children learn: through experience, through experimentation, through movement (trying something out for themselves such as the baby who comes to understand that they can make a mobile move by kicking it with their feet), through observation, through talk (adult:child and child:child) and through play (independent, collaborative, with an adult).

An outcome of the EPPE study (Sylva *et al.* 2010) suggested that effective early years settings have a staff with expert knowledge on how small children learn. When the early years practitioner has an understanding of the particular needs of babies and children under three, when there is an understanding of how this age group learns, then planning can become the flexible and responsive tool suggested above. The first book of this series, *Appropriate Environments for the Under Threes*, looks in some detail at key areas of development of this age range. An overview of those different aspects of development will be helpful here to further set the context for appropriate planning for this age group, and will incorporate specific examples drawn from practice and research to exemplify the significance of the practitioner's knowledge of child development throughout the planning process. The different ways of learning outlined above will also be incorporated into each of the six key areas. Whilst each area is outlined briefly here, it is important to bear in mind that all areas of learning and development are equally important and inter-connected.

Six key areas of development

1. Cognitive

The outcome of cognitive development is thinking, however a young child's ability to think is a process that develops over a prolonged period of time. This is because of the gradual and orderly changes that must occur to ensure their thinking processes become more complex and sophisticated. Piaget, Bruner and Vygotsky all developed cognitive development theories, each emphasising different areas and ideas in relation to a child's development. In addition, both Piaget and Vygotsky were regarded as constructivists. A constructivist approach is one which regards the individual as an active learner who constructs and internalises new concepts, ideas and knowledge based on their own present and past knowledge and experiences; in other words, the learner develops their own hypotheses and builds new knowledge based on what they already know. Following this line of argument, learning is not a phenomenon which is fixed and inert, but which is continually developing.

Babies and children under three as active learners

Newborn babies arrive ready to see and hear and experience all they can, and are capable of independent, intelligent thought from birth.

Example 1
Carefully chosen mobiles and later baby gyms are an important part of a child's first environment.

Activity

1. Look at the baby mobiles you have in your setting. Why did you choose these particular mobiles?
2. Now look at the baby mobiles from the child's perspective (i.e. from underneath).
- What is attractive about the mobile for the baby?
- What does/can the mobile do?
- What does the baby see/hear/experience from the mobile?

How can baby mobiles support a baby's early cognitive (thinking) development?

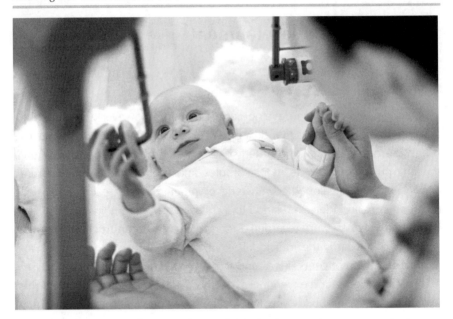

Figure 3.1 Supporting active learners 1

Example 2

At some point (usually about the age of six months or so), babies will learn to sit up. This may happen before they learn to crawl and should be considered as a great step towards independence because being able to sit up frees a baby's hands to explore and experiment, as well as encouraging risk-taking when reaching for toys. Babies will be intrigued by the toys and objects that surround them. They will touch, shake and chew them as they learn what they are about and what they will do. ('If I shake this will it make a noise like this one in my other hand does?' for example.) I remember the first time one of my children, Maisie, attempted to attach two Duplo bricks together at the age of six-and-a-half months. She had previously observed her older brother and sister (aged two years two months and three years seven months respectively) at play with the bricks. Having observed them and the potential of the bricks she was ready to have a go herself. This is an example of the Vygotskian principle of children learning from interactions and conversations with significant others from their families or wider social circles, including their peers. In this case Maisie's siblings were the catalyst enabling her to translate cognitive thought processes into personal action and experimentation and hence, subsequent learning. The early years practitioner must give toys and objects with an intelligent purpose; rattles that make interesting sounds, for example, and toys with different textures (plastic, wood, material).

Figure 3.2 Supporting active learners 2

Activity

What would Maisie's cognitive thought processes have been as she sat amongst the Duplo and attempted to attach two bricks together that day?

Implications for planning

Children learn to make sense of their world from birth. They are effective and motivated learners, building up knowledge through experience and learning to understand cause and effect in relation to what they can do and what they can get other people to do (Jarvis and Lamb 2001). They know that crying means that someone will attend to them, for example, and pointing to something means that it is likely to be handed to them. As they grow a little older they are then able to use the known action of pointing along with a rudimentary vocabulary of words such as 'drink', 'juice', or 'want!' Taking a constructivist perspective under the cognitive development umbrella puts the early years practitioner in the privileged position of scaffolding a child's learning from birth, facilitating and enabling development to take place.

2. Brain development

The responsiveness of the child's brain during the first three of four years of life should not be underestimated. Strong and lasting memories occur during this time; it is these early experiences which critically shape who they are as teenagers and adults (Gammage 2006, p.237). Interactions with adults leading to predictable, responsive (child-centred) care are important to the child's developing brain; neglect, abuse, and stress can have the opposite effect, causing harm (Zambo 2008). Children need to develop trust in their world.

Example of predictable, responsive care: sleep and rest

> Provision should be made (space or partitioned area) for children who wish to relax, play quietly or sleep, equipped with appropriate furniture. This may be converted from normal play space providing children can rest and/or sleep safely without disturbance. Each child should have their own bed linen, flannel and hairbrush if they are used (these may be provided by parents or providers). Sleeping children should be frequently checked.
>
> (DfES, 2007, p.35)

Babies need sleep; this is a fact. Sleep enables growth and consolidation; it is a restorative process that also allows muscles, bones and skin to grow, injuries to heal, recovery from illness, and the development of a strong immune system to fight off sickness. Sleep rests the brain, but at the same time activates it, allowing growth and enabling babies to remember what they learn, to develop increasing concentration skills, to solve problems and develop their thinking skills.

Implications for planning

The key worker approach supports a pattern of care that allows for close relationships between carer and child to develop. This in turn supports a planning process that responds to individual needs. It is important to record care patterns on a daily basis (see the Figure 3.3).

Figure 3.3 Example of a recording sheet for 0–2-year-olds (adapted from DfES, 2007)

Name Date	Abdul		
Activity	Comment		
Today I played with...	My favourite cuddly rabbit, the trolley and bricks (outside), the pine cones in the dry sand and the animal hand puppets with Jill [Abdul's key worker]. We listened to some of the nursery rhymes from 'Clap Hands Baby' and Jill taught me some actions to Hickory, Dickory Dock.		
I drank my milk	Time: 9am Amount: 6 floz Time: 12pm Amount: 5 floz Time: 3pm Amount: 8floz		
I drank my water/ juice	I drank 1 cup of water in the morning and 1 cup of juice in the afternoon (I asked Jill for juice: I said "juice, juice, juice").		
I ate...	Some banana at snack time, and all my lunch – pasta, sauce and salad. I got very excited because it was my favourite pudding today – icecream ("'scream!").		
My nappy was changed...	**Time** 9am 11.30am 2.30pm 5pm	**Wet/soiled** Wet Wet Wet Soiled	**Comment** Normal
I slept/rested...	For 2 hours after lunch I had a rest and a cuddle with Jill mid-morning.		

Reviewing provision for sleep

1 Do you have an area in your setting where babies can relax and rest and sleep when they need to?

2 Are you following patterns/routines of sleep established at home?

3 Is the baby always settled by their key worker to provide consistent and sensitive care?

4 Can the baby's key worker recognise signs indicating tiredness, thus being able to respond appropriately?

5 Does the key worker know how baby likes to be settled for sleep; reading a favourite story for example?

3. Language development

An appropriate environment for communication and language development is one in which the potential for talk has high status. Babies are born with characteristics which predispose them to be successful language learners. It is important to understand however that language experiences from birth play a significant role in language development. The significance of the way that adults interact with the child at this time should not be underestimated. Children who are not exposed to environments conducive to developing their language and communication skills appropriately are likely to have problems with social, emotional and cognitive development. Whilst there are many reasons why children may have problems learning language, a poor linguistic environment in the early years setting should not be one of them. The way practitioners communicate with babies and young children is therefore a very important part of their role. During the first three years of life, children are:

* developing their knowledge and understanding about how language works;
* developing a range and variety of vocabulary to use;
* learning to speak coherently and with clarity to make themselves understood;
* learning to speak with confidence.

Communication development needs to have a high priority in terms of planning, to include the organization of the day and, also, the practitioner's time.

Jarvis and Lamb (2001) examined the role of adult–child interaction in the communication development of children under two. Taking a set of twins as a case study, strategies used by the family to support the children's language development were identified; strategies which the authors suggest could be used in care settings where early years practitioners may be working with children under two in small group contexts. These strategies are outlined towards the end of this section, however the rationale for their argument is that key workers are often working with more than one child. It is a fact that children will not learn the function of communication without a more experienced language user to interact with; thus how can the key worker spend appropriate amounts of time with each child to ensure they receive adequate attention so that language skills securely develop? Jarvis and Lamb (2001) argue that early years practitioners need to be aware of why they are using particular language strategies. Adults are not always conscious of the language they are using with children; they do however tend to have an innate response to young children, simplifying their language accordingly, a concept known as 'motherese' or Child-Directed Speech – we have all heard the way adults speak to babies, for example, and know how we might adjust our talk ourselves.

Babies and children under three as competent language users and learners

Example 1: Communicating via early language

It is important to remember that in the first year of life babies are extremely interested in the sound of the human voice and in watching the face of a speaking person. The practitioner can feed the baby's interest in language (and prepare for later spoken language) by speaking clearly; it is unwise, although tempting, to raise your voice to an unnatural pitch for example. Model the correct use of language with children; if a child holds up their beaker and says, 'Juice!' put the word into a sentence – 'Yes Abdul, you are drinking your juice!' The early years practitioner can engage in conversation with a baby in the following way: when the baby makes a sound, imitate it. Eventually, the baby will purposefully begin to make sounds for the adult to imitate and will try to imitate sounds they make.

Example 2: Language and literacy: an emergent perspective

When we look at literacy from an emergent perspective, it begins from birth (see Bradford and Wyse 2010, for example); emergent literacy concerns 'children's individual literacy learning trajectories and the stages they go through as they progress towards conventional literacy' (Makin 2006, p.267). Makin looked at language interactions during shared book reading between 10 babies aged 8–12 months, and their mothers. The babies in Makin's study were defined as being in the 'prelinguistic stage', communicating through paralinguistic gestures such as vocalisations, body language and gestures, and facial expressions.

What happens when an adult shares a book with a child? What are children learning from the experience and what is the adult doing to support that learning?

1   The adult reads, holds the book the right way round, talks about the story, turns the pages, perhaps points to the illustrations. Makin (2006) found that mothers used literacy-related terms such as 'book' and 'page' with their babies. Later the baby begins to turn the pages themselves. Practitioners

reading this book can no doubt recall the child they have sat with to share a story who dictates or tries to dictate the pace; either by preventing a page being turned because they want to look at the pictures a little while longer, in which case time can be spent asking questions and pointing out key vocabulary; or by turning the pages at a speed incommensurate with the adult reading the text. With regard to the latter suggestion, whilst the child might have developed a new-found skill which is accurate, i.e. page-turning, they have yet to develop the understanding of waiting until the text has actually been read. A simple, 'Oh wait a minute, I haven't finished reading that page yet!', in addition to modelling an example of correct and appropriate language use, will soon help the child to understand that they will be able to turn the page but not until the next part of the story has been read. This is an example of responding appropriately to a child in terms of their developmental progress with regard to knowledge and understanding of how a book works. In Makin's study babies were encouraged to help with page turning; and some mothers would talk about 'the last page' or 'the end'.

Through sharing books, the baby learns that:

a   books are worthwhile and exciting;

b   books contain information of one kind or another;

c   books have pictures in them, they are attractive;

d   books have pages that must be turned and there will always be a final page (think of the child who always double checks for themselves that there are no more pages and comes to understand that the story always ends the same way);

e   stories have a beginning and an end;

f   books provide an opportunity to be close to an adult, perhaps to have a cuddle and be comforted;

g   their key worker sees them as someone who understands language because the key worker talks with them as if they were competent language users;

h   they can use their language skills to communicate successfully with their key worker.

2   Makin's study revealed that both verbal and non-verbal strategies were used by the mothers to draw the attention of their babies to the text such as pointing to a picture and talking about it once they were sure that their baby was focused, naming an object for example. These are strategies the early years practitioner should be familiar with. The baby learns that:

a   books are meaningful;

b   books are about discovery;

c   books provide an opportunity to hear spoken language;

d   books provide an opportunity to learn about the conventions of language; how verbal and non-verbal skills are required for successful communication;

e   books provide an opportunity to respond to spoken language through interaction with another person.

3   When we read with babies, we use strategies to build language and cognition, such as labeling and modeling sentence structure, again another key finding in Makin's study. Children return to favourite books and should be encouraged to choose a book to be read to them. The early years practitioner needs to look out for responses babies make to books and build on those; so if a baby points to a giraffe, perhaps making a sound, the expected adult response would be something like, 'That's right, that's a giraffe. Look at his long neck!' (whilst pointing and moving your finger up and down the giraffe's neck on the page). Some books provide opportunities to link in with a baby's experience such as 'He's learning to walk, just like you!' The baby learns that:

a   books are about real-life meaningful experiences;

b   books are a good source of information;

c   books provide an opportunity to develop vocabulary and to learn conventional language skills;

d   they prefer some books more than others.

Sharing books is important, even at this very early age. The early years practitioner should understand that reading with a baby is not something that should be rushed or done out of a sense of duty; they should understand that they are helping to develop a lifelong love of books and of learning, fostering engagement and supporting children's active participation. They should also see sharing books as a valuable way of scaffolding a baby's language development.

Implications for planning

Jarvis and Lamb argue that 'the growth of language and communication requires a partnership between the child and the environment and ... the most significant part of that environment is the adult carer. Both child and adult work together to achieve mutual understanding…' (2001,p.129). Early years practitioners do need to be aware of the language they use and to be able to change it as necessary. They need to have a good understanding of the development of communication (see *Appropriate Environments for Children under Three*, the first book of this series, for a more thorough overview of language development) and the role of the adult in this process. Practitioners need to have the time and skill to be responsive to individual children and to follow a child's lead, rather than always taking the lead role themselves. Suggested strategies for developing and monitoring communication include:

- referring to children by their name before every interaction;
- singing simple rhymes whilst cuddling babies to support face-to-face contact and early listening to voices and sounds;
- using daily routines such as nappy changes and preparing lunch as opportunities to develop new vocabulary. Repetition in routines should involve repetition with words and phrases so that language has meaning and familiarity;
- supporting children to make choices to encourage their own identity and develop their language skills, for example, 'Jack, would you like cheese or ham in your sandwich today?'
- providing opportunities for all children to experience sustained interaction on a one-to-one basis with an adult who knows them well;
- ensuring there is time for all children to participate in group games and activities;
- ensuring all children have equal adult time even if they do not demand it.

Jarvis and Lamb (2001) suggest that practitioners should have the opportunity to observe and monitor each other's communication skills, thereby setting up a process of moderation through which practitioners are made aware of their own interactions with the children in their care and also of areas which could be developed further. Whilst the focus of this book is observation of children, this might be an area for further exploration within your setting.

4. Social and emotional development

During the first year of life, babies are in the active process of forming social relationships with others (David 2009). Research has further shown that the quality of a baby's early interactions has potential outcomes for the quality of future relationships. Babies and children under three thrive on regularity, predictability and consistency, both at home and in their early years setting. This should extend to include regularity, predictability and constancy of relationships. The key worker approach, where one person assumes overall responsibility for a child, not only enables consistency of provision within the early years setting, but also consistency of relationship. Key workers become specialists who understand and respond to individual babies' and young children's needs, both physical and emotional; they support developing social skills. The key worker is the person who knows the child well and is aware of all the special details of how they are cared for, helping them to feel cherished and able to express themselves fully, to relax and feel confident that they matter. The key worker becomes the child's safe, secure and consistent base to return to, physically and emotionally.

Example: The impact of the key worker on a child's motivation

Walsh and Gardner's (2005) study looked at indicators of high and low levels of motivation amongst adults and the ensuing impact on children and the learning environment. Using these indicators as a useful starting point for analysis they have been adapted and expanded with the 0–3 age range specifically in mind and are set out below.

High levels of motivation are in evidence when:

The early years practitioner:
- offers stimulating, relevant and age-appropriate activities;
- shows a high degree of interest and interacts appropriately, allowing the child/children freedom, choice and opportunities to be curious, explore and investigate;
- is cheerful and enthusiastic, interacting with children, able to maximise learning opportunities.

The children are:
- happy to be left in the setting;
- pleased to see their key worker every day;
- eager to participate in what the setting has to offer;
- energetic, enthusiastic, displaying a degree of curiosity and interest in their environment.

The environment:
- is spacious, airy, aesthetically pleasing;
- has a plethora of attractive and age-appropriate resources;
- is one which extends to both indoor and outdoor provision.

Low levels of motivation are in evidence when:

The early years practitioner:
- shows little interest in the children or their activities;
- directs them, dominating their activity;
- undertakes necessary care routines out of a sense of duty;
- initiates activities that are uninteresting, not age-appropriate or relevant to young children;
- offers little variety or choice;
- would prefer to interact with peers, chatting rather than paying attention to the children in their care.

The children:
- appear unhappy;
- are unusually quiet or miserable;
- are apathetic and unenthusiastic;
- seem to complete an activity out of obligation rather than interest.

The environment:
- is dull and lacking in character;
- resources tend to be routine and uninspiring;
- children have little opportunity to use the environment available.

Implications for planning

Appropriate planning to support the social and emotional development of babies and children under three is achieved from the basis a secure understanding of:

1 the importance of the quality of a child's interactions from birth with other adults, and
2 the role they therefore play in providing security and constancy as the basis to enable a child to develop a healthy, well-balanced perception of self.

10 pointers for self-reflection

Having read the indicators of high and low levels of motivation above, reflect on your own attitude within your setting using the questions and suggestions below as starting-points.

1 Do I enjoy working with this age group?
2 If the answer is yes, ask yourself am I motivational in approach? Look at each bullet point in turn relating to high levels of motivation and the early years practitioner. Write down examples of your own good practice to support each point.
3 If the answer to question 1 is no, ask yourself why this is. Are you unhappy in the setting? Would you benefit from a greater understanding of child development? If so, you need to ask your manager or leader to arrange some relevant training for you.
4 Do children enjoy my company?
5 If yes, ask yourself why; look at each bullet point in turn under the child and think about each of the children in your care and the relationship you have with them. Write down why you think you have such a strong relationship with them.
6 If the answer to the question in pointer 4 is no, ask yourself why you think this is. Do you lack confidence? Is there anything you could do to change how children perceive you? Would you benefit from a greater understanding of how to work successfully with this age group? If so, you need to ask your manager or leader to arrange some relevant training for you.
7 Look at the bullet points relating to the environment under high and low level indicators of motivation. Are there improvements you and your setting could make? (Book 1 of this series, *Appropriate Environments for the Under Threes*, gives a comprehensive overview of responding to these indicators).
8 Review your responses to the above questions with a trusted colleague. Perhaps you should suggest that they do the same reflective exercise first. Give constructive feedback on each other's responses. What do you do well? How could you improve/build on your practice? Try not to use this as an opportunity to have a moan about people you work with or your job – that is not the point of the exercise!
9 Decide on three next steps you are going to take in the light of your reflections. What do your next steps mean practically? Even if you are a strong practitioner you might still want to consider a training course to help develop your practice or keep your knowledge up-to-date, for example.
10 Be an active practitioner. Take the outcomes of this exercise to your next appraisal meeting. It will help shape the discussions and give you evidence to support your own decision-making process.

As children grow, as their language skills develop (verbal and non-verbal) they will need support to learn to interact constructively and appropriately with their peers and those around them. This aspect of development is represented in a front-loaded way in early years curricula, for example personal, social and emotional development is the first area of learning in the current Early Years Foundation Stage in England. It will retain its high profile status amongst communication and language and physical development when the new Early Years Foundation Stage comes into statutory effect in September 2012.

5. Physical development

Young children have a natural desire to make things happen and to work out how their world works. They use all their senses and apply their physical skills to objects of interest. Their learning grows from the explorations of being able to hold objects and to experiment with actions. Babies have a strong drive to use their bodies. Two- and three-year-olds learn a great deal on the move. Physical movement and skills do matter to young children's development; they engage in a great deal of physical play and experience sheer joy in using their skills. Physical development covers the important skills of using the body; children need space to move about and hone those skills, for example to walk, run, skip, climb, and jump. Skills such as these use the larger muscles in the body, an area often referred to as gross motor skills. Fine motor skills involve the development of hand-eye coordination and the use of smaller muscles such as those in the hand and fingers to develop grasp and grip. According to the Montessori approach to education, there is a relationship between the child's so-called mastery of movement and the development of a healthy self-image (Stephenson 1998).

Physical milestones in babies and children under three

A milestone in relation to physical development refers to the age at which most children should have reached a certain stage of development. Table 3.1 shows physical milestones with suggested resources to support physical development.

Table 3.1 Physical milestones in babies and children under three

Age	Physical development (gross and fine motor)	Some suggested play resources to support physical development
0–4 weeks	Lies on back with head on one side Primitive reflexes; sucking, stepping, grasping	Comfortable play mats Range of mobiles Bells and rattles for sound production
1 month	Unsteady head control Makes tight fists with hands Grasps objects as they touch the palm of the hand Head and eyes move together	Cuddly toys Range of rattles Range of mobiles
3 months	Much more steady head control Can lift head and turn when lying on stomach Kicks legs and waves arms Watches movements of own hands, plays with own hands Holds rattle for a few seconds if placed in hand May begin to roll over	Baby gym Musical toys (to encourage head turning in direction of sound) Range of rattles and other hand toys Cloth balls, soft blocks, teething toys
4 months	Uses arms for support when lying on stomach Turns from back to side Holds on to and shakes small items May reach to grab something	Comfortable play mats to explore Baby gym Range of rattles and other hand toys Cloth balls, soft blocks, teething toys
6 months	Sits with, sometimes without, support Rolls over Pushes head, neck and chest off floor with arms when on front Using whole hand in palmar grasp, passes toy from one hand to the other	Comfortable play mats to explore Range of rattles and other hand toys Board books Cloth balls, soft blocks, teething toys
9 months	Sits alone with support Can pull to standing Reaches out for toys when sitting May crawl or shuffle Pokes at small item with index finger Develops pincer grip to pick up small items Will take and hold a small grip in each hand – tendency to use a pincher grasp using thumb and fingers Lifts block but can only release by dropping	Stacking toys Mirrors Toy telephones Play centres

continued ...

Table 3.1 continued

Age	Physical development (gross and fine motor)	Some suggested play resources to support physical development
1 year	Stands alone and starts to walk holding on Mobile through crawling or shuffling Enjoys self-feeding and holds cup with help Picks up anything from the floor with a neat pincer grip Clicks two cubes together Puts cubes in box when shown	Small push toys Small pull toys Balls to throw Plain and interlocking blocks Jigsaw puzzle trays
18 months	Can walk alone Pushes and pulls toys when walking Can walk downstairs with hand held Tries to kick a ball, rolls and throws ball Squats to pick up objects from the floor Assists with dressing and undressing Can use a spoon Uses a delicate pincer grasp for tiny objects Holds a crayon in primitive tripod grasp and makes marks Turns handles Pulls off shoes	Small push toys Small pull toys Balls to throw Plain and interlocking blocks Jigsaw puzzle trays Simple puzzles with large interlocking pieces Stacking toys Dolls Puppets
2 years	Walks up and down stairs with both feet on one step Climbs on furniture Builds a tower of six bricks Uses a spoon for self-feeding Puts shoes on Draws circles and dots	Climbing frames (indoor and outdoor) Toys that can be pulled, including wheeled trucks with handles Toys that can be pushed such as trolleys and prams Toys which can be ridden Stacking blocks Range of mark making and art materials
3 years	Stands and walks on tiptoe Can kick a ball confidently Jumps from low steps Pedals a tricycle Can draw a face Builds bridges with blocks when shown Undoes buttons Threads large beads	Dressing up clothes Role-play boxes Trucks Garage Dolls and dolls house Range of blocks and construction materials Range of mark making and art materials

Implications for planning

The successful early years practitioner will plan for individual children knowing what they can expect to achieve physically and what they have already achieved thus far. Observed and recorded, that knowledge will feed into assessments and create the basis for future plans. Physical activity is not just about playing with toys, although that is important, but activities such as developing reach or learning that clapping hands together will make a noise, for example. It is about developing coordination; to this end physical development is often talked about in terms of fine and gross motor skills. Fine motor skills involve intense hand-eye coordination such as threading beads, or mark making. Mark making can however be experimented with on a gross motor level, for example buckets of water and large paintbrushes or rollers, the kind you would paint a wall with.

6. Play and development

'Children should have opportunities to experience much of their learning through well planned and challenging play' (CCEA 2003, p.7). Early childhood education is underpinned by a strong tradition which regards play as essential to learning and development, for example by setting the context for the development of communication and collaborative skills (Wood and Attfield 2005; Siraj-Blatchford 2009). From birth to one year children engage in sensorimotor or practice play: the repetition of a learned sensory or motor activity for the sheer pleasure of repeating it. At about the age of five months babies begin to play with objects. By the age of nine to ten months they begin to differentiate objects, preferring new to familiar objects which they handle in such a way as to gather as much information from them as possible. Object play becomes more mature from the age of two when objects tend to be used appropriately and incorporated within symbolic, or make-believe (fantasy) play. By the age of three children are highly imaginative and this naturally has a subsequent impact on their imaginative play. They begin to identify quite strongly with key adults in their lives, becoming increasingly interested in what they do and imagining themselves doing the same things; there is a marked increase in their dramatic play through which they act out adult roles for themselves, incorporating these within their play.

Identifying with adults: Simon's fire check register

At the age of just turning three years old, Simon was beginning to show an interest in mark making. He observed his key worker taking a register every morning using an A4 sheet and a clipboard. One morning he asked her if he could have his own clipboard and register. The key worker handed this to him. Simon began to look around the room and 'tick' children's names off his register. He then decided to dress as a fireman in a tabard and hat. His register became his fire check register and he made sure everybody in the room was accounted for, noting his observations on his board.

Activity

What would you plan for Simon next to support his learning through play? Consider:
1   What his interests are;
2   what his achievements are;
3   what his next steps could be. Think about different areas of the setting, including the outdoor area;
4   what activities could you set up for Simon?

Implications for planning

The best play resources for a child of any age capitalise on their developmental needs. For two year olds play resources that develop large or gross motor skills are most appropriate, for example. Go back to Table 3.1 on p.45 to see how play resources can be used to support physical development. The successful early years practitioner:

- will understand how children learn through play and be a playful person themselves;
- will have their own enthusiastic approach to play;
- will demonstrate such characteristics as smiling and laughing throughout play;
- will be willing to engage in play, comfortable to play games such as peek-a-boo.

In short, they will understand the significance of children learning through play and plan appropriately from that basis.

Learning: a summary

Walsh and Gardner's (2005) study evaluated the quality of early years classrooms from the perspective of the child's experience. Three categories were developed from which to measure that experience: academic, social and emotional. Nine key themes representing integral aspects of a high-quality environment for learning were further developed, relating to each of the three categories above as follows:

- academic (motivation, concentration, higher-order thinking skills and multiple skill acquisition);
- social (social interaction, respect); and
- emotional (confidence, well-being, independence).

Whilst Walsh and Gardner's study focussed on children aged between four and five years' old it is clear that all key themes should be considerations when planning for babies and children under three.

Activity

Read the following statements about learning.

- Learning has to be active.
- Learning includes repetition/practice/consolidation.
- Learning includes reprocessing spoken or written information.
- Learning involves thinking about thinking.
- Learning involves self assessment and reflection.
- Learning builds upon previous knowledge and work.
- Learning is individual.

Look at Table 2.1 in Chapter 2. What opportunities for the above ways of learning do the activities represented in each area of continuous provision provide?

NB. This activity could be undertaken as a whole staff exercise. Areas of continuous provision could be shared amongst staff members working in pairs before being fed back and discussed.

Table 3.2 Overview of the role of the adult with babies and children under three (DfES, 2007)

Age	Role of the adult
Birth–1 year	• Realise that just because a baby is not crying everything must therefore be fine. It is important to interact, talk and smile. • Repeat sounds and actions, imitate expressions, sounds and action for the baby to copy. • Encourage a more active role for babies aged 6 months and over, responding to them in the role of initiator. • Use changing, feeding and bathing times as opportunities to support curiosity. • Provide opportunities for the accessible exploration of everyday objects; place heuristic collections in baskets at ground level, for example. • Talk about what the baby can see, respond to their utterances, their efforts at communication, and describe what is happening for them. If a baby perceives themselves as able to communicate, then they will make attempts to do so.
1–2 years	• Extend play experiences, providing a commentary for the child. • Provide space and time to explore safely. • Provide a wider range and quantity of materials and offer opportunities for exploring the properties of those materials; • Provide opportunities for exploratory play. • Support emerging schema such as collecting, transporting, fitting into and through. • Provide opportunities to explore in and outside, including, where possible, trips outside the setting. • Be attentive so that the learning potential of experiences offered is increased. • Offer children a commentary in their actions, gradually increasing the complexity of language used. • Encourage role play; model for the children, for example, buying goods from a shop.
2–3 years	• Provide security when new people or experiences are encountered. • Provide the companionship of other children who can become partners in play. • Help children to build relationships with a wider range of adults in the setting. • Support children's interest in representing their widening experiences of the world by access to a variety of materials and toys. • Enable children to choose the experiences that match their interests and needs.

Chapter conclusion

Table 3.2 gives an overview of the role of the adult with babies and children under three at three broad age stages. Above all, learning is about the individual; when all planning is based on that individual and what they know it is appropriate. To exemplify this point, Atkinson (1989) looked at how French preschools aim to respond to young children by providing a 'tolerant and familiar climate [environment] in which each is valued as an individual, is encouraged in undertakings that express personal needs, and is appreciated in success and assisted in defeat' (p.77). Three key principles underlie the French pre-primary approach:

1   responding to observations of the child;
2   responding to the child's play; and
3   responding to the child's practical knowledge.

In addition, there is a dual nature to consider when responding to babies and children under three; the early years practitioner is both a caregiver and an educator. It is this child-oriented approach that is championed in this chapter, where the child is both the subject and the doer of learning. The early years practitioner's responses must be guided by children's overall development.

4 | Observation

Planning must be considered within the context of an ongoing cycle which includes observation, assessment and evaluation as part of a continuous process. This chapter asks why this process is so fundamental to children's learning and development. The planning cycle for babies and children under three includes observation as a key element, worthy of further discussion. Accurately recording the outcomes of an observation is looked at in terms of making a so-called valid judgement or assessment. The chapter looks at how to use observational information as the basis for planning environments, routines and activities that will enhance children's learning and development. The chapter elucidates how the use of a range of observation strategies can provide insights into children's social, emotional, physical and academic development.

Why observe?

Observation of children and their interactions can be used as precursors to effective planning and organisation, to individual assessments and in the identification of schema or pathways of learning (Broadhead 2006). Maria Montessori (1912) built a whole philosophy of education from observation alone, arguing that the child can only be free when the adult becomes an astute observer of behaviour; in other words, an accurate understanding on the early years practitioner's part of a child's needs enables appropriate development and learning to take place. A very brief exploration of her method sets the context for the benefits of observation. Claiming that her philosophy (the Montessori Method) was based on scientific observations, she felt that any action of an adult that was not a response to the children's observed behaviour would limit the child's freedom. This is child-led learning at its most optimum. Montessori claimed that her observations revealed that children learn through movement and play; that children enjoy learning in an environment designed to meet their needs; that children learn best through their senses; that children can read and write and count at an early age (bear in mind what is now known about emergent literacy and early mathematical development); that children respond to educational opportunities in an environment which is prepared to meet their needs; and that children often reveal a spontaneous self-discipline within a prepared environment. Whilst this book is not about the outcome of Montessori's observations it is still interesting to note them and to reflect on them in relation to principles behind good early years practice. Finally, observation can help to provide insights into a child's social, emotional, physical and academic development; areas that run in tandem with Walsh and Gardner's (2005) three overriding categories providing an insight into the quality of a setting's provision from the child's perspective.

The benefits of observation

Renck Jalongo *et al.* (2004, p.145) argue that 'keen powers of observation are fundamental to providing quality programs and competent preschool teachers use these thoughtful observations of children to provide relevant supportive educational experiences.' This means in practice that:

1   At its most basic level, observation helps to build knowledge about an individual child. Children's development is complex and variable; the key question is what can I see happening in relation to this child? As the early years practitioner gets to know individual children, certain patterns of behaviour will begin to make sense, for example in relation to a child's personality or interests, as well as in relation to expected milestones of development or developing knowledge such as the utterance of first words to name people or objects. Conversely, it is essential that the early years practitioner can identify if a child is having problems and needs extra support.

2   Effective scaffolding in the early years requires accurate observation (Broadhead 2006). Observation provides essential feedback and evidence from practitioner input and enables the practitioner to assess whether work with a child is effective or not. The outcome of observation from this perspective provides vital information that should directly feed into planning; key questions here include was/is the plan appropriate? Does it need to change? How? Why? What should be included in the plan? What

are the next steps I need to take to build on what this child knows/can do in order to inform my next plan(s)?

3 Observation provides a context for gathering evidence. It is important to remember that the early years practitioner cannot necessarily draw general conclusions from one observation, however children should be observed on more than one occasion in order to be confident about drawing general conclusions or reaching a judgement about their progress or difficulties in learning.

4 The interpretation of observational evidence can be supported through discussion with colleagues. Post-observation dialogue with colleagues is an integral feature of practice in the Reggio Emilia area of Italy, for example. Early years settings should place teamwork high on the agenda of priorities in terms of an approach to effective working.

5 Observation skills have to be learnt; they develop with practice. They will however be supported and enhanced by an individual's knowledge of development of babies and children under three; effective early years practitioners who are familiar with the curriculum and who have expert knowledge on how small children learn (Sylva *et al.* 2010).

6 Observation is about more than just watching; the practitioner is also noticing and thinking at the same time. You might, for example, watch a child building with bricks, but notice how the child fits them together; what they are doing with them or how they are held in the hands. What happens if another child approaches? Is there a reaction? Is the new child ignored? Acknowledged in any way?

7 Observation supports the building up of evidence to reveal patterns of behaviour or ability over time. It is important not to jump to conclusions when recording something that is seen for the first time.

Learning through play: the place of observation

Broadhead (2006) argues that observing play involves time. Time is needed to see how children's play develops and to observe how their ideas and problems are created and solved within and through play. Depending upon the age and circumstances, play will sometimes occur alone and sometimes with others. Within the domain of play, the importance of extended and repeated observations will support a trajectory of repeated preferences or themes that emerge. This is one strategy that can support a child-led agenda of learning through play through identifying a child's interests.

It's time to play!

1 During a setting staff meeting, divide into pairs or groups of three. Choose a play resource from the setting. Consider the following, making notes:
   - What would/could children learn from playing with the resource?
   - What aspects of learning would you want to observe and record? Why?
   - How would/could you know that learning was taking/had taken place?

2 Use the resource within your planning and observe at least one child interacting with it during a session.
   - What did they learn from playing with the resource?
   - What aspects of learning did you observe and record? Why?
   - How did you know that learning was taking/had taken place?

3 Compare both sets of notes. Were your predictions accurate?

4 How will undertaking this exercise help you when approaching future observations?

Recording observations

It is worth noting that Wertfein et al.'s (2009) study noted that documentation and observation of a child's development is one of five key aspects for the reported high quality of education in early childhood infant–toddler centres. According to Sylva et al. (2010), qualification in observation and documentation of child development leads to positive outcomes in these fields. The need to use accurate language to record observations is imperative; it is explored here in relation to the objective and subjective statements outlined in Table 4.1.

Remember that all observations should be dated, include times, and should include the child or children's name(s). Ways to record observations include using diaries and dated notes (especially if the objective is to look for patterns over a period of time), narrative accounts (timed, open-ended, or critical incidents), checklists, charts, rating scales, diagrams such as maps and drawings (to show a child's movement and interactions in the setting, for example), photos, video and audio recordings.

Table 4.1 The language of recording

Subjective judgement	Comment	Objective, observable fact	Comment
She has good communication skills.	What is this statement actually telling us?	She can express herself in complete sentences, for example, in the role play grocery shop outside she turned and said to me, 'I went shopping with mummy yesterday'.	Note that these observation notes provide a context for what the child said.
She can concentrate for long periods.	What is meant by a 'long period'? What was the child concentrating on?	She spent ten minutes building a tower with the Duplo bricks (see photograph).	The context for the observation is clear, and has been recorded using an additional format. It will provide good evidence for the child's Learning Journey or in a profile.
He has good manipulative skills.	No context or explanation of what is meant by 'good manipulative skills'.	Today he threaded 10 beads on a lace, using his finger to count each bead from 1 to 10 in order.	Strong evidence to suggest that the child is secure in counting from 1–10 and understands one-to-one correspondence.
He shared appropriately.	What/how did he share appropriately?	He took turns with C to turn the pages 'Duck in a Truck' which I read to them today. I supported them with gentle reminders of whose turn it was to turn the page.	The observation gives accurate information about the child's ability to share appropriately with one other child and with adult support.

Activity

Consider the following statements. What kind of additional information is needed in order for them to make sense and become objective, observable facts?

1 Alana was happy today.
2 Sally kicked Karl twice this morning.
3 Jay spent about 20 minutes building a cave at the sand tray.
4 Devlin was fascinated by the water wheels in the water tray.
5 Jerome can kick a mobile with his foot.

In your setting: What are you going to do to change the Why? and How? to ensure you are recording observations accurately and clearly using appropriate language and formats (i.e. the language of recording).

The quality and usefulness of observational evidence varies in relation to its focus, timescale and context. It is important to establish reliability (through accurately observed and unbiased recorded evidence) and validity (a defensible connection between the description of what is visible to the early years practitioner in the observed behaviour and what is assumed is inferred). Observation data may be quantitative (How many…? How frequently…? How long did he/she spend…?) or qualitative (What happened when…? How did they…? What he/she said during…). Often a combination of these approaches is needed to provide reliable and accurate information.

Observing children's development: developing meaningful contexts for observation

The possibilities for observation in each area of learning are endless, however Table 4.2 can be used as a starting point for thinking about physical, social and emotional, and language development in babies and children under three. What should the early years practitioner be looking for in relation to each developmental area?

Table 4.2 Starting points for physical, social and emotional and language development

Observing physical development	Observing social and emotional development	Observing language development
• How does the child move about? • Are movements appropriate for the child's age? • Can they co-ordinate their movements? • How do they move/use the space they are in? • How do they use large equipment? • How do they manipulate and use small equipment?	• How does the child behave in everyday situations? • How does the child express feelings and emotions? • How does the child relate to other children? • How does the child relate to other adults? • How confident is the child to explore? • How confident is the child with other children and/or adults?	• How does the child attempt to communicate? (gesture? sound? speech?) • What non-verbal cues can I see? • What vocabulary is the child using? Is this appropriate for the child's age?) • How does the child respond when spoken to by another child? • How does the child respond when spoken to by another adult?

Activity

Using Table 4.2, look at the planning you have developed for the coming week for one of your key children and make sure that you observe them in each of the three areas. Develop an observation schedule that includes some or all of the suggested questions. Are there any additional questions that you need to include? Write your responses as fully as you can on your prepared schedule.

What does this information tell you about the child? Write a summary for each area (NB. the summaries will be returned to in Chapter 5).

Chapter conclusion

The early years practitioner must be sensitive to the child's choices and efforts – the value of the individual must be a primary focus. Piaget described children as 'intellectual explorers' (1970, p.51); they must therefore be listened to and responded to. Atkinson argues that 'if our educational interventions are guided by children's observations, play, and expressions of how they understand what they are experiencing ... we will be successful in our efforts to provide early childhood programs that are "healthy" for young children' (1989, p.85). This chapter has argued for the importance of observation with regard to supporting the early development of babies and children under three. It has looked at the value of observation in relation to different elements of development and given thought and consideration to the language of recording, which must be accurate and contextualised in order to be of optimum value and use.

5 Observation and planning: making the links

This chapter practically demonstrates what can be done to develop appropriate planning and observation techniques for children aged between 0–3 within the context of the early years environment. It looks at how observation feeds into planning in order to ensure success for the child. The quality and usefulness of observations are revisited and explored in the light of discussion in the previous chapter. Examples of approaches to planning are set out and the intrinsic relationship between planning and observation further highlighted in relation to the overall planning cycle within successful early years environments. The chapter compares principles behind planning from a global perspective, examining Italy's Reggio Emilia and New Zealand's Te Whaariki early years frameworks.

An overview

All the planning and preparation involved in an activity will be wasted if one vital element is ignored: has the child reached the required stage of development in order to be able to participate fully in this activity? In other words, do they possess the skills necessary in order to take part in it, enjoy it, and succeed at the activity? Most activities are planned with the aim of extending or developing children's existing skills, but those skills will not be extended or developed if the child is not ready for that next step; at the risk of repeating a previous example from Chapter 1, there is no point giving a child a twenty-piece jigsaw if all they have mastered thus far are six-piece tray puzzles. This is where the role of observation comes in both as a regulator and predictor of a child's ability and achievement. Effective planning as a result of effective and accurate observation will make all the difference to the success of an activity.

It is insufficient preparation to simply look at a child development chart to develop plans from. Whilst such a chart will have its place in providing reassurance for the early years practitioner and in supporting judgements made, it should be looked at within the context of an inherent knowledge of what the practitioner is aware an individual child can already do through observation and time spent with them. When planning, the early years practitioner needs to do so with an awareness of the acceptable range and recognised limits within the different areas of development. Within the framework of overall patterns of expected development, the rate and sequence of development will be unique to each individual child. This is where observation plays a key role, providing evidence and information for the practitioner to enable appropriate activities to be developed that promote opportunities through knowledge of the individual; activities that acknowledge, support, develop and embrace each child's ability, their skills, their culture, their interests, and their care needs.

Planning activities

Planning for unstructured activities

This type of planning occurs when an adult provides an activity for a child to experience in their own, open-ended way. The outcomes may be very different from the intention of the adult. An example of this type of planning might be developing a water play activity by putting spiders, jugs and a piece of plastic drainpipe in the water tray. The adult might be thinking that the rhyme 'Incy Wincy Spider' could be sung whilst using the resources in a hands-on way – they may even model this with the child. Yet the child may only be interested in investigating capacity, filling and emptying the jugs, whilst at the same time entranced by the flow of the water and the sound that can be made as it is poured back into the tray.

Planning for structured activities

A structured activity will be planned by the practitioner with a specific learning outcome in mind. A cookery activity may be used as the basis for investigating change processes, for example. Cookery activities often happen with small groups of children participating and there are many opportunities to incorporate learning outcomes in relation to personal, social and emotional development;

Using the unstructured play scenario write down your responses to the following questions:

1   What could the focus of your observation be?
2   What would the child be learning through responding to the activity in this way?
3   What developmental skills are being learned and/or developed? (Think carefully about the language you use here; begin with hand-eye coordination, for example and think about where this fits in to the physical curriculum).
4   What potential is there for language skills to be developed?
5   How might the outcome of this activity be building on previous learning or experience?
6   What would you plan next as a result of your observation? (NB. You might want to think about elements such as the properties of materials as well as thinking about developmental skills).

personal hygiene or self care through washing hands; learning to take turns, for example when weighing and adding ingredients or stirring the mixture. Language skills will be involved, for example developing breadth of vocabulary though describing change processes in response to open-ended questions such as 'What has happened?' or 'What do you think will happen to our mixture when we add the flour?' and using key vocabulary such as 'recipe', 'weighing scales', and 'mixing'. Cookery activities are a good way to visually support key words. Additionally, for children who are finding it difficult to integrate with their peers, an individual learning objective involving learning to be part of a group may also be appropriate. Finally, cookery activities also provide opportunities for physical development; practising fine motor skills and hand-eye coordination through weighing, mixing, icing, and placing, for example.

Experiential activities

An experiential activity is one where a child finds meaning through direct experience; experiential activities essentially encourage and support exploration. Learning is achieved through a personal response within the environment, both

Promoting cultural differences and equal opportunities: points to consider when planning group activities

- *The interests of all children should be met in an activity.* Consider each child in your group individually. What is the purpose of the activity? Ask yourself how each child will benefit from the activity. What will each learn?

- *Carefully consider how all children can join in.* Is one of the children in the group shy or timid, for example? How will you encourage participation? Do you have a child with a hearing impairment? How will the group communicate with you and with each other?

- *Consider which cultural background(s) you need to take into account.* Research those cultures in depth; begin from the premise that diversity should be celebrated. Think of ways that you can promote positive images of different cultures; what about books, for example? Ensure children do not feel excluded; a story that concentrates on a family setting with both parents at home perhaps needs to be balanced with stories depicting one-parent families. Develop resources within the setting that represent different cultures such as play food, cooking utensils, dolls and puppets. A Bangladeshi baby doll will be of far greater support and comfort to the young Bangladeshi child coming to terms with a new sibling through role play than a white one, for example.

- *Develop an awareness of festivals across the faiths.* Put major festival dates in the setting diary and enjoy making clay lights at Diwali with the older children, for example, or painting some Chinese characters at Chinese New Year (what a fantastic opportunity to develop young mark making skills). Do be sensitive when approaching planning however; Muslim families do not celebrate Christmas, for example, and neither do Jehovah's Witnesses.

within and beyond the early years setting, to expected or unexpected activities; it is 'the process whereby knowledge is created through the transformation of experience' argues Kolb (1984, p.41). Dewey described experiential learning as learning that takes place when a person involved in an activity is able to look back and evaluate it, determine what was useful or important to remember, then use this information to perform another activity. Experiential activities provide opportunities for learning by doing or learning through experience. An example of experiential learning would be baking gingerbread biscuits from scratch, rather than eating ready-made biscuits and describing how they are made. The child would then understand that certain ingredients need to be mixed together to create an end product for example, a principle that can be applied to making other types of food to eat; or that change occurs when certain things are mixed together, a principle that could be extended to observing what happens when water is mixed with soil for example, which is why the younger child may say 'I'm cooking' when experimenting (experiencing learning) in this kind of way!

Thematic activities

Thematic activities (sometimes referred to as topic planning), take a realistic activity relevant to a child's experience to provide opportunities to develop in several or all areas of the curriculum, for example a trip to the local park or a role-play area such as a post office within the setting. A thematic plan is often split into the various areas of the curriculum or areas of development to ensure a range of suitable activities are provided.

Planning activities: key considerations

For babies and children under three there are several umbrella needs to consider when planning; a comfortable, safe environment, consistent care routines, close

Activity

Develop a thematic plan based on a recent experience the children in the setting have enjoyed. You should make this age-/room-appropriate.

and loving relationships, inclusion and equal access, communication and the opportunity to play. It is important to understand that within each need there are many variations according to the individual child. The secret to good support is through planning that responds to each individual child's needs; thus the clear link between observation and planning. The main premise for planning for the early years practitioner is to always plan from the position of a thorough knowledge of all the children in the group.

Consider the following:

* *Begin with what the child can do*; planning should build on a child's successes and develop from the perspective of achievement.
* *Develop a thorough knowledge of the resources available in the setting*; children learn best when resources are commensurate with their developmental stage.
* *Look at the child holistically*; the early years practitioner will need to take into account physical and emotional, as well as intellectual or academic needs.
* *Look at the curriculum holistically*; for this age range, the curriculum is presented as an integrated way to learn. Children use various skills across curriculum areas; learning about numbers involves speech, for example. Personal, social and emotional development comes into nearly every aspect of learning for children of this age, whatever the activity.
* *When planning for a group of children ask yourself what are the individual needs of each child?* Two children of the same age are likely to be very different from each other; their stages of development may differ. They may have different interests or preferences; for example their dietary requirements may differ. They are also likely to have very different personalities. Finally parental considerations or wishes which are to be taken into account may also be very different.

On any planning sheet (see Figure 5.2) the early years practitioner must make sure you that they have taken into account sufficient considered evidence to show how the following has been taken into account:

* The needs of each individual child.
* How they intend to adapt the activity to support the needs of every individual child.
* Where the activity will take place. Does the group need space to move around? To be quiet? Indoors? Outdoors?

Figure 5.1 Promoting independence

- Provision of equipment suitable for all the children.
- Whether special equipment needs to be provided for certain children.
- Whether equipment can be reached by all the children to promote independence. Even babies need to be able to kick a mobile under a baby gym for example, or reach for a rattle from a sitting position!
- Whether any of the children require practical support.
- What support will need to be given to encourage inclusion amongst the group. What observation skills will need to be used to ensure everyone is fully participating?

As a marker of how clear any plan is, it is useful for the early years practitioner to think about it from the point of view of someone who is taking over from them at very short notice – due to illness, for example. Would that person be able to clearly understand and follow the plan?

A global dimension for planning

How does the early years practitioner ensure planned provision in the light of observation and assessment? Any approach to planning must be contextualised

Figure 5.2 Adult-guided/focus activity planning sheet: what needs to be included?

Date:
Name of staff:
Area(s) of Learning:
Learning intention(s):
Opportunities for Assessment:
Target children:
Resources:
Experience/activity:
Adult input (include key vocabulary and key questions):
Differentiation (how will you meet every child's needs?):
Evaluation (to inform future planning and in addition to individual observations, continue on back of this sheet):

within the established framework of an appropriate quality curriculum for babies and children under three, and the potential impact of such a structure in relation to enabling young children to thrive. In recent years many countries in Europe have revised existing early years curricula or introduced new frameworks, reflecting 'recent changes in ideas about children's learning, effective pedagogy and the role of early childhood education and care in society' (Wertfein *et al.* 2009, p.19). Oberhuemer (2005, cited in Wertfein *et al.* 2009, p.19) argues that there is general agreement that early childhood curricula should meet the child's needs, interests and individual dispositions to learn. Because life experiences in early childhood are very variable, the curriculum should follow the child. What are the implications of such an approach in relation to planning? An exploration of what this means in practice now follows, drawing on the Reggio Emilio approach to planning and New Zealand's Te Whaariki approach to planning.

Reggio Emilia

Principles underlying the Reggio Emilia approach to early education are rooted in the theories of Dewey, Piaget and Vygotsky amongst others, thus reflecting a constructivist perspective. A constructivist approach is one which regards the individual as an active learner who constructs and internalises new concepts, ideas and knowledge based on their own present and past knowledge and experiences; in other words, the learner develops their own hypotheses and builds new knowledge based on and building on what they already know. Following this line of thinking, learning is not fixed and inert, but continually developing. A socio-cultural viewpoint is also paramount to the Reggio Emilia approach, a viewpoint also rooted in the work of Vygotsky. Vygotsky argues that children are guided into increasingly mature ways of thinking by communicating with more capable others and through interactions with their surrounding culture. Socio cultural theory incorporates three key features:

1   A child's learning is developed and supported through the involvement of a more experienced other, often an adult, although the concept does extend to siblings and peers. Social interaction with a more competent member of society enables cultural knowledge to be transmitted to an individual who in turn is able to internalise and incorporate new ideas and concepts into their existing repertoire.

2   The significance of a social context for development. Development, in terms of young children's strategies for and attitudes to learning, depends on a

combination of interaction with (more experienced) people and tools that a particular culture provides to help children form their view of the world.

3   Knowledge is constructed as a result of the child's active engagement with the environment. It is through such active engagement that a child's thinking develops, as a result of their ability to assimilate and internalise the processes and practices provided by their socio-cultural context. The understandings that children develop as a result of their socio-cultural background form part of what Bourdieu (1986) calls 'habitus'. Habitus is the lens through which each of us interprets and relates to the world.

Applying theory to practice, the Reggio Emilia approach seeks to solicit multiple points of view regarding children's needs, interests and abilities; therefore parents, teachers and children *all* play a role in contributing to the determination of school experiences. Curriculum planning and implementation revolve around open-ended and long-term projects that are based on the reciprocal nature of teacher-directed and child-initiated activity. Teachers thus often work on projects with small groups of children, whilst other children engage in a wide variety of self-selected activities typical of pre-school settings. Looking at the principle of open-ended and long-term projects from a socio-cultural perspective, it makes sense that project topics are also selected on the basis of academic curiosity or social concern on the part of teachers or parents, or serendipitous events that direct the attention of the children or teachers.

Observation and planning the Reggio Emilia way

The Reggio Emilia curriculum is further characterised by features such as real-life problem-solving amongst peers along with numerous opportunities for creative thinking and exploration. The projects that teachers and children engage in may derive directly from teacher observations of children's spontaneous play and exploration. Skills and methods of observation must therefore be developed to play a central role in the Reggio teacher's overall pedagogical repertoire. The Reggio Emilia approach aims to promote a more flexible and personalised teaching method; Reggio teachers place a high value on their ability to improvise and respond to children's predisposition to enjoy the unexpected, for example. Successful projects are considered to be those which generate a sufficient amount of time, interest and uncertainty to provoke children's creative thinking and problem-solving and are open to different avenues of exploration; adult supported, child-initiated and child-led.

Projects begin with teachers observing and questioning children about the topic of interest. Based on children's responses, teachers introduce materials, questions, and opportunities that provoke further exploration of the topic. While some of these teacher provocations are anticipated, projects often move in unanticipated directions as a result of problems children identify. As projects progress, children are deemed to be generating and testing their hypotheses (the constructivist perspective) and are encouraged to depict their understanding, developing outcomes through mediums such as drawing, sculpture, dramatic play, and writing. Children are encouraged to work together towards the resolution of problems that arise. One of the principles behind the Reggio Emilia approach is trust; teachers trusting themselves to respond appropriately to children's ideas and interests, trusting children to develop their own paths of learning, and trusting parents to be informed and interested contributors to their children's educational experience.

The ultimate aim of the Reggio Emilia approach is for every child to receive an education best suited to their needs, interests and abilities. Teachers develop their understanding of the learning processes of all the children they teach, including children of different genders, abilities and cultures. Reggio Emilia supports an ethos where children work in partnership with other children, as well as with their teachers and parents.

Te Whaariki

Te Whaariki, the early years curriculum framework for New Zealand, stresses the importance of inclusion, the child as a unique individual (including the celebration of culture; note that the document is written in two languages, English and Maori, the two main cultures of New Zealand), the value of working with parents, and the importance of play. Te Whaariki is a holistic curriculum, based very much on a socio-cultural perspective; 'the curriculum is provided by the people, places, and things in the child's environment: the adults, the other children the physical environment, and the resources' (Ministry of Education 1996, p.11). With this context in mind, the curriculum is envisaged as a mat or 'whariki', woven from principles, strands and goals outlined within the framework as a whole, but individualistic to each child in terms of what their socio-cultural background or influences bring to the setting. The child is therefore encouraged to develop very much as an individual, beginning from 'where they are at' and what they know.

Observation and planning the Te Whaariki way

Following on from the importance of the child as an individual (the uniqueness of each child), Te Whaariki considers the whole child when observing and planning for them. Every part of the curriculum interrelates and connects, an ethos reflected in the planning process. Experiences, activities and events may be based on forward planning, or they may evolve in response to a particular situation. Parents are invited to be included in the planning process as much as possible. The emphasis is on identifying a child's disposition to learn rather than having to work towards a set of pre-defined outcomes; this is in direct contrast to the approach in England where currently a child works towards a pre-prescribed set of Early Learning Goals in six areas of learning outlined within the Early Years Foundation Stage in England, for example. Generally, the starting point for planning is through observations of the children; their interests and needs form the foundations of all planning. Plans are adapted on a day-to-day basis leaving flexibility for an emergent curriculum and opportunities for 'teachable moments'. In terms of recording outcomes, portfolios are developed which document a child's progress to include for example a range of learning stories, work samples, video clips (on a CD), photos, contributions from parents, and comments from the children. The idea is to build a broad and balanced picture of a child's learning and development in the setting rather than marking or grading progress against a pre-defined curriculum goal.

It is the responsibility of each early childhood setting to plan its own programme to enable achievement of the goals of each strand in the Te Whaariki. There are five strands in total; Well-bring, Belonging, Contribution, Communication, and Exploration. The idea is that each early childhood setting will be unique, developing their own distinctive pattern for planning, assessment and evaluation; 'planning the curriculum whariki should be a continuing process, involving careful observation, identification of needs and capabilities, provision of resources, assessment, and evaluation' (Ministry of Education 1996, p.28). Discussion amongst setting staff is encouraged to ensure that there is a clear rationale and justification of a given approach, beliefs and practices. Planning usually begins from observation of the children's interests, needs and behaviours (dispositions). A focus for planning involves care routines such as planning for mealtimes. Finally, planning 'should help adults who work in early childhood education to understand what young children are learning, how the learning happens, and the role that both adults and other children play in such learning' (Ministry of Education 1996, p.28).

For self-reflection

This exercise encourages the setting to spend some time comparing and contrasting principles behind Reggio Emilia practice with the setting's approach and is probably best undertaken as a staff team. What can be learnt? Begin with the following set of questions:

1   Which theoretical principles underlie current practice in the setting?
2   What could you incorporate within current practice to develop a constructivist approach to children's learning? Is this approach helpful? Why/why not?
3   What could you incorporate within current practice to develop a socio-cultural approach to children's learning? Is this approach helpful? Why/why not?
4   How can you identify a child's interests? How do you know what they are?
5   What do you understand by the term 'serendipitous events?' Describe some serendipitous events that have happened at the setting recently, either for individual children, groups of children, or the setting as a whole. How can such events be incorporated within your planning?
6   What examples of real-life problem solving have you observed recently?
7   How can observation lead to a more flexible and personalised teaching method for children?
8   How could you further develop your skills and methods of observation and documentation to respond to children's experiences?

Individual setting staff
1   How confident are you in improvising and responding to a child's predisposition to enjoy the unexpected? What holds you back?
2   Do you trust yourself to respond appropriately to children's ideas and interests?

Thinking about parents
1   How involved are parents' views as you approach developing your plans?
2   Does the setting as a whole welcome and create a partnership with parents?

For further self-reflection

Compare Reggio Emilia with Te Whaariki.

1   What similarities can be drawn between the two early years curricula?
2   Is there anything else that you can now add to your previous reflections?
3   What links can you make between features of Reggio Emilia and Te Whaariki in relation to principles behind observation and planning outlined in this chapter?
4   What are the key principles behind the planning process in your setting?
5   How could you develop your principles behind good practice in relation to planning following this chapter content?

Activity

Using the observations and summaries collated in response to the final activity in the previous chapter in response to Table 4.2 (see p.59 for the table and for a reminder of the activity), *what are the next steps for planning for this child?*

Consider the following:

* the child's interests
* their response to the activities you observed them undertaking
* stages of development
* what the child knows
* what the child needs to know
* the child's care needs

In the light of your considerations, plan some appropriate activities for the child to follow on from your observations. What will the focus for your next observations and assessments be?

Chapter conclusion

This chapter has focused on key principles behind planning and implementing activities to enhance development designed to support and encourage children to communicate and develop their thinking through their play and learning activities. It has explored the challenge of planning appropriate activities for babies and children under three alongside consideration of their individual care needs and links with developmental progress. The chapter has explored principles behind practice from a global perspective, examining planning and observation in Italy's Reggio Emilia and New Zealand's Te Whaariki early years frameworks.

Planning and observation: towards a review of practice

This chapter suggests ways forward for reviewing a setting's practice in terms of what needs to be in place in order to plan and observe effectively as an early years staff to meet the developmental and learning needs of babies and children under three. Issues will be covered such as staff training (it has been pointed out earlier in this book that observation skills can be practised and improved). Such a review may feed into elements of the setting development plan. When reviewing practice, settings must be confident in their own judgements resulting from such an exercise. In this instance, the outcome has to be one of knowing that planning provision equates to that which constitutes and supports every child's unique developmental and learning needs. Many settings undergo this approach of a reflective, progressive review on an ongoing basis.

Reviewing provision: a starting point

Every setting should have an established set of planning tools. These are core documents to record all elements of planning; long-, medium-, and short-term planning, including weekly overviews, indoor and outdoor plans and daily activity plans. An established set of planning tools such as these should adequately meet the needs of the setting. All members of staff should adopt the same approach to planning, including using the same core documentation, in order to ensure consistency of provision.

Planning documentation

Following the line of argument set out above, every setting will need to develop their own set of planning pro formas. These may differ across the setting depending upon the age of the child (babies will need a different format from a 2- or 3-year-old); however it is always advisable to use a consistent set of planning sheets. These might include:

- long-term plans
- medium-term plans
- short-term plans:
    - weekly planning sheets for the indoor environment
    - weekly planning sheets for the outdoor environment;
    - adult-focus activities (one-to-one and group);
    - a planning sheet for outings.

Any plans should be written on the basis that they may need to change as a result of response (the activity may not be stretching enough as well as perhaps being too ambitious for a child), or because of unforeseen circumstances such as a fire drill, or because of other factors such as a child becoming unwell or even equipment breaking or failing. Plans do not necessarily need to be beautiful, word-processed documents, but rather documents that have room for annotated comments showing children's responses and reasons for change, thus reflecting a flexible approach amongst practitioners.

For self-reflection

Look back at your planning from last week. In what circumstances did you need to change routines or activities? How did you adapt existing or planned routines and activities?

Appropriate resources

It is helpful for every member of a setting involved in planning to have access to lists or inventories of resources available to incorporate within their plans. These need to be divided into categories; water play and sand play, for example. It is a good idea, depending upon how your setting is organised, to categorise in

Reviewing current practice

At a staff meeting conduct a review of all the current documentation used for planning. It might be helpful to look back at the section in Chapter 2 entitled 'What is the practitioner planning for? Key elements of planning for babies and children under three' (p.15).

- Is everything included on the plans that should be there to support and pinpoint every child's development and learning? If not, what needs to change?
- Does the structure of the plans change depending on the age of the child (plans for babies will look very different from three-year olds, for example)? If not, what needs to change?
- Consider the structure of the planning tools you use. Do the forms need to be reformatted in any way?
- Make sure all the forms are available electronically for every member of staff to access.

Making changes may not be achievable in one meeting alone. Developing planning may be something to add to the setting development plan and reviewed as part of an ongoing concern; in fact this is the more likely outcome as any reformatted planning sheets will need to be evaluated and reviewed over a period of time.

relation to age or room; but do remember outdoor resources as well. You may also have a range of resources for all members of staff to access from a central point. Here are some further suggestions for categories:

- story books and information books relating to various themes/topics
- story books with CDs for listening
- mark making materials
- art materials
- modelling materials
- messy play
- wheeled, sit-on materials
- construction kits
- small world play
- role-play

- dressing-up
- musical instruments
- ICT.

You can probably think of many more! Resource lists can be made available in a planning file for all members of staff involved in the planning process. Taking such an approach will:

1   ensure a wide range of appropriate resources are used at all times as part of the setting's continuous provision;
2   ensure that practitioners know at a glance what resources are available to support children's interests;
3   ensure that practitioners know at glance what resources are available/ appropriate to support children's learning;
4   ensure that practitioners know at a glance what resources are available/ appropriate to support children's stages of development.

An extension of this approach might be for a setting to then link areas of the curriculum that support various resources, for example, physical development and wheeled, sit-on vehicles.

Planning behind the planning: setting development and resources

It goes without saying that access to a wide range of age-appropriate resources is important for babies and children under three, however it is also a fact that every early years setting must work within a specified budget and the more likely scenario is that resources will build gradually over time as an ongoing concern. Resources do not always have to be expensive; many natural resources such as shells and pine cones can be gathered from the immediate environment, for example. Appeals can be made to parents and carers for items. Many practitioners will tell you of their innate tendency to pick up resources as and when the opportunity arises; not necessarily because it is something they are particularly looking for at the time. My rather extensive shell collection came from a day trip to Felixstowe; sets of shaded colour charts cost me nothing at a DIY store to be used over and over for paint mixing activities. There are of course some resources that have to be bought; play mats, baby gyms, mobiles, sit-on vehicles, to name but a few.

Reviewing resources

- Building on your inventory of resources that you as a setting have, can you identify any immediate gaps in provision?
- Is there an area of provision in terms of age-appropriate resources that would benefit from being included immediately within the setting development plan?
- Realistically, what proportion of the setting budget can be allocated to the upkeep of resources?
- With regard to the older children in your setting, look at your long-term plans; do you have everything you need to support the proposed themes/topics? What could you do to fill in any gaps? Do resources necessarily have to be bought?
- How can you as a setting best utilise what you do have to ensure equality of access to resources?
- Would your setting benefit from a resource coordinator or resource coordinators? Resource coordinators might for example be assigned responsibility for a particular age group and/or a particular area of learning.

Observation pro-formas

In addition to coordinating planning to ensure a consistent approach throughout the setting, a similar approach is wise with regard to observation. Developing a set of observation pro-formas will further enhance coordinated provision and provide points for discussion and reflection amongst the staff team.

Supporting planning and observation: considerations for babies and children under three and their parents

An important element of the role of the early years practitioner should be to value and support relationships between parents and children (Parker-Rees 2007, p.13). It is important for settings to create viable links with home experience, to exchange information and respond to parents' needs and preferences with

Figure 6.1 An example of a simple observation pro-forma

Date:
Child:
Context:
Activity (child-led/focus):
Observation:

regard to babies and children under three. Routines are extremely important for this very young age group and consideration must be given with regard to the regular structure of the day, within which the early years practitioner will need to incorporate and plan for care routines, as well as play and learning activities.

Observation, accurate judgements, and recording the developmental progress (language, physical, and personal, social and emotional development) of babies and children under three involve vital skills on the part of the early years practitioner. To this end it is vital that every early years practitioner has a clear understanding and secure knowledge of early childhood development. What can be done to support developing setting practice from the basis of such a secure knowledge base? Parker-Rees (2007) suggests that focused observation

Reviewing current practice

Chapter 4 suggested different ways to record observations. These included:

* diaries and dated notes
* narrative accounts (timed, open-ended, or critical incidents)
* checklists
* charts
* rating scales
* diagrams such as maps and drawings
* photos
* video and audio recordings.

Consider each of the above and ask the following questions:

1 Would this method of observation be appropriate for this setting?
2 If yes, what would it achieve? When/how would the setting use this method of observation?
3 What would need to be included on a pro-forma for this method of observation? Is a pro-forma necessary?
4 What happens to the observation once it has been undertaken? Where does the information go?
5 How will this method of observation be used to feed into planning? Could there be another purpose for this observation?

of babies' interactions with familiar adults in the home environment might help in developing early years practitioners to see and feel what babies can achieve, given optimum support; conversely direct, personal experience of the close, familiar relationship which allows parents to understand and support their young children may also contribute to a greater respect for parents.

Reviewing current practice

- Does your setting incorporate home visits before a child begins at the setting as part of current practice?
- What is/would be the value of this kind of visit?
- What does/would the practitioner notice within the home environment?
- Are there any notes/observations that could be taken during this visit? What would be the nature of these?
- If you do not already have one, would it be helpful to develop a pro-forma for members of staff to take with them during a home visit?
- Do members of staff need to write an additional reflective observational account of aspects of the visit? What would be the nature of these?
- How does/could information gleaned from a home visit feed into setting provision? Consider for example the current home-setting policy, the planning policy, potential implications for current provision.

Planning and observation: final considerations for effective early years practice

A key worker approach to organising appropriate care for babies and children under three is a consistent premise in relation to lines of thinking discussed throughout this book. Above all, babies and children under three need to be cared for in an environment in which adults are available, tuned in to their needs, responsive to their needs, and consistent in their response and approach; in other words, they need to be cared for by skilled individuals who understand them. As such, in order to become that skilled individual, the key worker needs to consider, and be considered for, ongoing training in order to continually develop and embed early years knowledge and understanding as part of an inherent early years practice. Planning skills and observation skills can be taught and are important components of many current early years training programmes. A range of options should be considered for every early years practitioner within the setting, from recognised certificates and levels to day conferences and refresher courses. A programme of development will also include whole staff training sessions.

Chapter conclusion

This chapter has set out suggested ways to move practice forwards in relation to planning and observation as part of an effective, ongoing, and reflective approach to setting development. It has looked at practical issues in terms of the paperwork involved in planning and observation and making such paperwork purposeful and supportive of practice. Practical suggestions have been made to support and develop the planning cycle supported by reflections on current practice with a view to change within the setting, both immediate and longer term.

7 | Drawing the threads together

This summary chapter looks at some of the considerations for planning alongside developmental and learning needs. Suggestions are made in relation to planning and observation in the light of this information and some practical suggestions are outlined on which the early practitioner can choose to draw. For babies and children under three, it is important to incorporate care routines such as regular times for nappy changes and sleep within an overall umbrella of activities to develop an ever-increasing independence.

Planning and observation for babies and children under three

Birth to 1 year

Babies use all their senses to explore and respond to their immediate environment, making sense of what they see, hear, feel, touch, and smell. Visual stimulation is vital in the first year of life. Remember that a baby sees life in black and white for the first four months. A great deal of neurological and anatomical development takes place as babies lie on their backs and tummies, playing with their feet and working on rolling over, for example.

Observe:
The ways babies find out more about themselves and their environment through use of their senses.

Figure 7.1 Visual stimulation is vital in the first year of life

Plan:

Times to join in with babies' explorations; fingers and toes, for example. Sing rhymes and familiar songs to support their exploration in learning about their bodies and the environment. Look at books together; a wide range of tactile books are now available for babies which tap into their immediate experiences and which support the development of rhyme. Talk to babies about their world and what happens within it; they are listening to you, readily tuning in to the voice of a familiar adult. Babies need to be rocked; this is a motion they find soothing and stimulating. Plan opportunities for rocking and swinging, movements (which support the neurological development of balance and co-ordination). Once a baby is crawling provide a range of surfaces to support different tactile experiences and on which to develop movement skills. Observe how, as the baby moves from one surface to another, their attention is drawn to the contrasting sensation of each one and look for the change in how they need to use their body to navigate them. Develop opportunities for heuristic play using everyday objects such as empty cardboard boxes.

Learning and development:

- the world I live in is safe and secure;
- the world I live in is interesting and is opening up for me;

- I am surrounded by people who care about me and who take care of me;
- I can communicate with those around me and they respond to me;
- I have some space to move around in (in my cot, on my play mat, for example);
- I am learning to move within those spaces (kicking, reaching, touching, for example).

Summary of the adult role

- Recognise the importance of repeating actions and sounds, imitating expressions, actions and sounds for the baby to copy.
- After the age of 6 months, encourage babies to develop a more active, initiating role.
- Use changing and feeding and bathing times as opportunities to interact with babies. This will give the practitioner an opportunity to use non-verbal as well as verbal communication in a constructive, positive way to promote self-esteem.
- Understand that visual stimulation is vital. Non-mobile babies need to be put in positions that give them plenty to look at, reach for, to bat and to grasp; provide opportunities to explore objects and sounds, for example mobiles, by putting them within reach. Carry them to interesting places both indoors and outdoors.
- Provide opportunities to explore everyday objects in an accessible way, for example, in baskets.
- Talk with the baby about what they see and respond to their utterances.
- Develop opportunities for sensory experiences.

1 to 2 years

As mobility increases, young children tend to express themselves through physical action and sound.

Observe:
The movements and sounds made as young children explore the space around them, experiment with musical instruments, and investigate materials such as paint, dough, and glue. Look for preferences, and note the development of physical skills such as hand-eye coordination and skills such as pulling and pushing.

Some suggested sensory experiences

Children between the ages of 0–3 need to experience their world using all their senses:

- bubbles;
- water – add colour and scents along with a range of different resources (a shipwreck in blue water; a crocodile swamp in green water, complete with foliage from the garden; jugs and containers to explore capacity);
- soap flakes mixed with water;
- cornflour mixed with water (gloop) – colour can be added;
- investigate a range of materials – foil, scarves, bubble wrap, etc.; lay these on the floor for babies to crawl over and for toddlers to walk over;
- investigate jelly;
- freeze water (sometimes with objects inside such as Arctic animals for example) and leave thawing in the water tray;
- make feely bags containing items of different textures such as feathers, shaped beads, and leaves;
- hand/foot/finger painting;
- add sand and glue to paint to change the texture
- small musical instruments such as bells and shakers;
- plants with a range of textures and smells such as grasses, lavender and rosemary;
- indoor and outdoor surfaces with a range of textures to crawl and walk over such as grass, bark, rugs and play mats.

Plan:

Opportunities to use materials such as paint (including finger painting) and dough to support sensory exploration and 'messy play'. Build on children's interests and preferences and allow time for concentration and exploration. Provide protective clothes for babies where necessary. Children of this age will need plenty of opportunities to master the ability to clamber, go up and down, to swing, spin, slide and bounce. They will want to collect objects in bags or baskets, in addition to experiencing and handling an object. Now that they

Figure 7.2 Developing hand–eye coordination

are walking their hands are free to manipulate, to fill and empty, to lift and carry, to push and pull. They want to move as they master motor control and coordination.

Learning and development:

- my ability to communicate using my developing language skills is getting better. I have people around me to communicate with who know and understand me;
- I am given time and space to explore a range of interesting and stimulating resources available within the setting;
- an environment has been created for me that responds to my individual needs;
- my coordination is developing; I am learning to walk. Sometimes I fall over or bump in to things because my sense of balance is still developing;
- being able to walk frees me up to use my hands in exciting ways.

Summary of the adult role

- Extend the length of play episodes, offering an increasingly complex commentary on what is happening as language skills develop.
- Provide a large enough space and time to explore safely.
- Provide a wider range of materials for exploration of properties.
- Provide opportunities for exploratory play.
- Provide opportunities for both indoor and outdoor experiences.
- Be attentive so as to optimise learning and development opportunities, record key observations.
- Encourage role play; children learn by copying the actions of the adults around them, for example, going shopping.

Role play: going to the doctor

Resources to include:

- a receptionist's desk with a booking-in diary and pencils, a keyboard, a phone;
- a waiting area with magazines and health leaflets, posters on the wall, a selection of toys for children (include a small world play ambulance and doctors, for example);
- signs, for example open/closed, no mobile phones;
- medical resources such as bandages and slings;
- medical equipment such as a stethoscope, a blood pressure pump, weighing scales, a first aid box, a thermometer;
- dressing-up clothes – doctor's jacket, nurse's hat, a green shirt, name badges;
- photographs of a real doctor's surgery along with information and story books about going to the doctor;
- photographs of the children in the role play area.

2 to 3 years

As children become more skilful in using language and other forms of communication (dance, music, art, for example), they begin to comment on the activities they participate in and the resources they access and play with.

Observe
Patterns of thought or movement (schemas) revealing how new situations are created through play such as transporting sand or water from one area to another. Record the language being used to describe experience.

Plan:
A range of activities to support every child's unique and individual perception of the world. Follow the child's lead and try to avoid imposing your own adult perceptions on an activity; provide resources such as tins, boxes, boxes and corks and note how the child uses them to support heuristic play. Begin to ask questions as they immerse themselves in their self-chosen directions. Include some group activities to support the ongoing development of relationships with peers.

Learning and development:

* learning is set in meaningful contexts for me;
* I am free to learn through doing;
* my world is rapidly moving beyond the realm of myself and I am learning ways to accommodate the presence of others;
* my developing language skills mean that I can communicate with my peers as well as the adults around me.

Summary of the adult role

* Provide security when new people or experiences are encountered.
* Provide the companionship of other children (partners in play).
* Help children to build relationships with a wider range of adults in the setting.
* Support children's interests through access to an appropriate range of resources.
* Enable children to choose an experience that matches their interests and needs.

Final thoughts

This book has considered the role of planning and observation within the context of appropriate provision for babies and children under three based on their unique developmental and learning needs. Within the age range lies a vast range of potential for development over a relatively short period of time. At the same time this is a vital time for development, and experiences count in these very formative years (Sylva et al. 2010). It is the committed early years practitioner who draws on their knowledge of child development and who can see and respond to every child as the individual that they are, developing activities that allow for progress and which optimise children's outcomes. Underpinning this approach to practice will be the core role of observation to inform planning as part of high-quality provision which begins with the child.

References

Alexander, R. (ed.) (2010) *Children, their world, their education. Final report and recommendations of the Cambridge primary review.* London: Routledge.

Atkinson, A.H. (1989) French pre-primary education: a tradition of responding to children. *Early Child Development and Care* 46(1): 77–86.

Bourdieu, P. (1986). *Distinction: a social critique of the judgement of taste.* London: Routledge.

Bradford, H. and Wyse, D. (2010) Writing in the early years. In D. Wyse, R. Andrews. and J. Hoffman (eds), *The Routledge International Handbook of English, Language and Literacy Teaching.* London: Routledge.

Broadhead, P. (2006) Developing an understanding of young children's learning through play: the place of observation, interaction and reflection. *British Educational Research Journal* 32(2): 191–207.

Burchinal, M., Roberts, J., Nabors, L. and Bryant, D. (1996). Quality of center child care and infant cognitive and language development. *Child Development* 67(2): 606-20.

CCEA (2003) *The revised Northern Ireland primary curriculum foundation stage.* Belfast: CCEA.

David, T. (2009) Young children's social and emotional development. In T. Maynard and N. Thomas (eds), *An introduction to early childhood studies* (2nd edn). London: Sage.

DfEE (2002) *Birth to three matters.* London: QCA.

DfEE (2005) *Curriculum guidance for the foundation stage.* London: QCA.

DfES (2007). *Statutory framework for the Early Years Foundation Stage.* Nottingham: DfES.

Featherstone, S. (ed.) (2008) *Again! Again! Understanding schemas in young children.* London: A&C Black.

Gammage, P. (2006) Early childhood education and care: politics, policies and possibilities. *Early Years* 26(3): 235–48.

Jarvis, J. and Lamb, S. (2001) Interaction and the development of communication in under twos: issues for practitioners working with young children in groups. *Early Years* 21(2): 129–38.

Knight, S. (2011) *Risk and adventure in early years outdoor play.* London: Sage.

Kolb, D.A. (1984) *Experiential learning: experience as the source of learning and development.* Upper Saddle River, NJ: Prentice Hall.

Makin, L. (2006) Literacy 8–12 months: what are babies learning? *Early Years* 26(3): 267–77.

Ministry of Education (1996) *Te Whariki.* Wellington: Learning Media Limited.

Montesorri, M. (1912) *The Montessori method: 1912 edition.* New York: Frederick A. Stokes.

NICHD Early Child Care Research Network (2006). The interaction of child care and family study of early child care and youth development. *American Psychologist* 61(2): 99–116.

Nutbrown, C. (2011) *Threads of thinking schemas and young children's learning* (4th edn). London: Sage.

Nyland, B. (2000) Early childhood literacy: babies, context and participation rights. Paper presented at the AARE Conference, Sydney, December.

Oberhuemer, P. (2005) International perspectives on early childhood curricula. *International Journal of Early Childhood* 37(1): 27–37.

Parker-Rees, R. (2007). Liking to be liked: imitation, familiarity and pedagogy in the first years of life. *Early Years* 27(1): 3–17.

Piaget, J. (1970). *Structuralism.* New York: Harper & Row.

Renck Jalongo, M.R., Fennimore, B.S., Pattnaik, J., Laverick, D.M., Brewster, J. and Mutuku, M. (2004) Blended perspectives: a global vision for high-quality early childhood education. *Early Childhood Education Journal,* 32(3): 143–55.

Siraj-Blatchford, I. (2009). Early childhood education, in T.Maynard and N. Thomas (Eds.). *Young children learning.* Oxford: Blackwell Publishing.

Snow, C.E. and Van Hemel, S.B. (eds) (2008) *Early childhood assessment: why, what, and how.* Washington, DC: National Research Council.

Stephenson, S. (1998) *The joyful child: from birth to three years.* Arcata, CA: The Michael Olaf Montessori Company.

Sylva, K., Melhuish, E., Sammons, P., Siraj-Blatchford, I. and Taggart, B. (2010) *Early childhood matters. Evidence from the effective pre-school and primary education project.* London: Routledge.

Tickell, C. (2011). *The early years: foundations for life, health and learning.* London: HMSO.

Walsh, G. and Gardner, J. (2005) Assessing the quality of early years learning environments. *Early Childhood Research and Practice* 7(1): 1–17.

Wertfein, M., Spies-Kofler, A. and Becer-Stoll, F. (2009) Quality curriculum for under-threes: the impact of structural standards. *Early Years* 29(1): 19–31.

Wood, E., and Attfield, J., (2005). (2nd ed.). *Play, learning and the early childhood curriculum.* London: Sage.

Zambo, D. (2008). Childcare workers' knowledge about the brain and developmentally appropriate practice. *Early Childhood Education Journal* 35(6): 571–7.

Index